AF422369

THE CO-LIVING SOLUTION

How to Maximize Profit with Purpose through Affordable Housing

A Real Estate Investor's Guide to
Building a Profitable Co-Living Portfolio

MACARENA GARCIA

COPYRIGHT

DISCLAIMER

By reading this book, you acknowledge and agree that the author and publisher shall not be held responsible for any decisions you make or actions you take based on the information provided. All investment decisions involve risks, and past performance is not indicative of future results.

DEDICATION

To my parents…

Your journey as immigrants was marked by immense sacrifices, yet you carried each challenge with grace and determination, never once voicing a complaint. You promised me the world, and through your unwavering support and boundless love, you encouraged me to chase my dreams fearlessly. This book is a testament to the strength, resilience, and dedication you've shown every day. Thank you for paving the way and believing in me—I couldn't have done it without you.

TABLE OF CONTENTS

FOREWORD

A Timeless Playbook for Building a Purpose-Driven and Profitable Co-living Portfolio
By Atticus LeBlanc

The affordable housing crisis isn't just a headline—it's a brutal reality affecting millions of Americans. I've spent 16 years in the trenches addressing this challenge as an affordable housing developer and operator. As the founder and CEO of PadSplit, the largest co-living marketplace in North America, I can tell you firsthand that co-living isn't just another investment trend. It's one of the most practical solutions we have for solving our national housing shortage while generating sustainable returns.

Let me put this in perspective. In 2021, there were 36.2 million single-person households in America and roughly 61% of them – that's 22 million individuals – couldn't qualify for a median-priced one-bedroom apartment. These aren't just statistics; they're nurses, teachers, construction workers, and other essential workers who keep our communities running. They're the exact people getting priced out of traditional housing options.

That's why Macarena García's *The Co-Living Solution* arrives at such a critical moment. This book isn't just another real estate investment guide – it's a practical blueprint for investors who want to be part of the solution while building sustainable wealth.

What makes this book particularly valuable is its focus on the nuts and bolts of successful co-living operations. Renting by the room is more profitable than traditional leasing models in almost any market – but it's also significantly more complex. Macarena breaks down these complexities into actionable strategies, from market selection to legal compliance, financing structures, and operational best practices.

At PadSplit, we've seen how shared living transforms lives and creates wealth. When thoughtfully managed, co-living reduces housing costs by pooling resources while also building community resilience. Macarena's work aligns perfectly with this philosophy. She highlights how investors can become part of the solution by providing affordable housing options while securing financial independence for themselves.

I'm particularly excited about Macarena's focus on empowering women investors in this space. This isn't just about diversity for diversity's sake – it's about capitalizing on the unique perspectives and skills that women often bring to real estate investing, particularly in community-focused models like co-living.

For investors reading this book, understand that you're looking at more than just another real estate strategy. The co-living market represents a $184 billion annual opportunity when you consider just the single-person households who can't qualify for traditional apartments. But beyond the market opportunity, you have the chance to be part of a solution to one of our nation's most pressing challenges.

Whether you're a seasoned real estate investor or just starting out, this book provides the roadmap you need to enter the co-living space successfully. Macarena's insights, combined with real-world examples and practical strategies, offer a comprehensive guide to building a profitable, sustainable co-living portfolio.

The future of housing won't look like the past fifty years. As demographic shifts continue and housing shortages persist, co-living will play an increasingly important role in our housing ecosystem. This book shows you how to be part of that future – and how to do it right.

One room at a time,
Atticus LeBlanc
Founder and CEO, PadSplit

INTRODUCTION

" The secret of getting ahead is getting started. The secret of getting started is breaking your complex overwhelming tasks into small manageable tasks, and starting on the first one."
— *Mark Twain*

What if I told you that right now, there's a golden opportunity waiting for you to take control of your financial future—an opportunity that allows you to make a real difference in your community while also building wealth? It's an opportunity that many women are missing out on simply because they don't know it exists or because they believe real estate investing is a man's game. Let me tell you: it's not.

The world of real estate is evolving, and women like you and me are leading the charge, especially when it comes to solving one of the most pressing challenges we face today: affordable housing.

Welcome to *The Co-living Solution: How to Maximize Profit with Purpose through Affordable Housing.* My name is Macarena García, and I'm here to show you how co-living can transform your real estate portfolio, your financial independence, and your ability to help others—all while building wealth.

Whether you're a seasoned investor or just starting, this book is your roadmap to identifying, purchasing, renovating, furnishing, and operating affordable co-living housing in the United States. And trust me, this isn't just about financial gains. It's about empowering yourself, creating opportunities, and contributing meaningfully to the solution for affordable housing.

Why Co-Living?

Why co-living? What's so special about this trend, and why should you invest your hard-earned money into it? Let me start by saying this: co-living is more than just a buzzword. It's a practical, scalable solution to the affordable housing crisis affecting cities across the United States.

As housing costs skyrocket, more and more people are seeking affordable living options. That's where co-living comes in. It's a model that not only fills the gap in affordable housing but also offers an incredible opportunity for real estate investors, particularly women.

When I first started investing in real estate back in 2009, the market was reeling from the housing crash. It was a scary time for many, but for those of us who saw the potential, it was also a time of opportunity. I didn't have the knowledge or the network I have today, but I took that leap. Fast forward to 2024, and I now own eleven rental properties in my name and three others in partnership with fellow investors.

Along the way, I've also become a private money lender, and I'm proud to say that I've helped other women get their start in real estate. Since late 2022, I've completed 13 loans, and I can tell you from experience that real estate—especially co-living—offers rewards beyond just financial returns.

The best part? You don't need to have all the answers before you start. I certainly didn't. What you do need is the drive to take action, a willingness to learn, and the right guidance. That's precisely what I'm here to give you with this book. My journey hasn't always been smooth, but every step has taught me something valuable—and I want to share those lessons with you.

My Journey into Co-Living

My adventure with co-living began in 2023 when I listed my first co-living property on *PadSplit*, the leading marketplace for co-living properties in the United States. If you're unfamiliar with *PadSplit*, they focus on creating affordable, community-oriented housing solutions in cities that desperately need them. PadSplit has even highlighted some of my *properties* as model homes. To be recognized for the quality of my co-living spaces was a tremendous honor, but it also reinforced something I've always believed: real estate investing isn't just about making money—it's about making an impact.

Early on, I realized that co-living wasn't just a way to generate income but a way to help people. By providing affordable housing, I was offering a solution to a growing problem while creating opportunities for myself and others. Owning a property and renting it out for a profit is one thing. It's another thing entirely to know that the space you've created gives people a sense of stability, affordability, and belonging while also solving the housing crisis.

This journey into co-living taught me a lot, and that's why I have been coaching women real estate investors on mastering the co-living strategy and why I decided to write this book. I want to share everything I've learned, from my successes to the mistakes I've made along the way. I want you to be able to avoid the common pitfalls and fast-track your way to building a successful co-living portfolio. I've had the privilege of connecting with the right people at the right time, and now I want to pass that knowledge on to you.

Why Women Should Lead in Real Estate Investing

Now, let's address something that's been on my mind for years: why aren't more women leading the charge in real estate? Women are natural problem-solvers. We're great at managing people, fostering relationships, and creating powerful networks. And yet, too many of us shy away from real estate investing. We assume it's too difficult, too male-dominated, or too risky.

But here's the truth: women are uniquely positioned to succeed in this space. We can see the potential in properties that others might overlook. We manage with empathy, innovation, attention to detail, resilience, and relationship building, making us ideal leaders in the co-living investment space. I've seen firsthand how women excel in real estate, especially in the co-living sector, where fostering a sense of community is essential.

By stepping into real estate investing, you're not just securing your financial future—you're contributing to the solution of one of the biggest problems of our time: affordable housing. You'll provide homes for people who might otherwise struggle to find affordable options. You'll be creating opportunities for others, and you'll be making a tangible difference in your community.

The Reality of Affordable Housing in the United States

We can't talk about real estate without acknowledging the housing crisis. Across the United States, housing prices are skyrocketing, particularly in major cities. Millions of people struggle to find affordable homes, and this problem isn't going away anytime soon. As an investor, this presents a unique opportunity—because where there's a problem, there's also potential for innovation.

Co-living is one of those innovations. It's a solution that addresses both affordability and the growing demand for community-oriented living spaces. More and more people, especially younger generations, are looking for affordable, flexible housing options that offer more than just a roof over their heads. They want a sense of belonging, a place where they can connect with others—and co-living provides precisely that.

Through this book, I will show you how to tap into this demand and turn it into a profitable, sustainable business. You'll learn how to identify suitable properties, finance them, renovate and furnish them for co-living, and manage them effectively. By the end of this journey, you'll be ready to build your co-living portfolio and have a solid plan for making it work.

Why This Book Matters Now

There's never been a better time to dive into co-living. The demand is growing, the market is ripe for innovation, and investors like you are ready to step up and take the lead. This book is your guide to making it happen.

You don't need millions of dollars or decades of experience to succeed. What you need is the right mindset, the right strategies, and the willingness to take that first step. In the chapters ahead, I'll share everything I've learned over the past 15 years—from the challenges to the triumphs—so you can avoid my mistakes and create your own path to success.

This book isn't just a how-to guide—it's a call to action. Women can reshape the real estate industry, solve the affordable housing crisis, and build wealth for themselves and their families. All it takes is the courage to get started—and that's precisely what I'm here to help you do.

Are You Ready?

So, are you ready to take control of your financial future? Are you ready to build a real estate portfolio that generates income and makes a difference? If you're excited about the possibilities, then let's dive in. Together, we can solve the affordable housing problem, one co-living property at a time.

CHAPTER 1

THE RISE OF CO-LIVING IN AFFORDABLE HOUSING

---

*"What counts in life is not the mere fact that we have lived.
It is what difference we have made to the lives of others that will
determine the significance of the life we lead."*
— *Nelson Mandela*

Affordable housing has become a growing concern across the country, but here's the thing: every crisis presents an opportunity. You and I are at a pivotal point in real estate, especially when providing solutions that help people afford a place to live without draining their savings. This is the moment for women entering real estate to make a mark and truly make a difference.

If you've ever thought about diving into affordable housing, I'm sure the sheer complexity of the market might feel overwhelming. But here's where co-living steps in—a model that addresses affordability and speaks to the human desire for dignity, stability, and belonging. In this chapter, we will explore how co-living is rising as a game-changing solution in the affordable housing space. And I will show you why it matters, especially for us as women investors. You're going to walk away from this chapter with a deeper understanding of co-living, its power, and how you can shape the future of housing.

Defining Co-Living and How It Differs from Traditional Rental Properties

Co-living represents a paradigm shift in how we think about and approach shared living arrangements. At its core, co-living is a modern adaptation of communal living that addresses affordability. Understanding what co-living truly means and how it differs from traditional rental properties is essential for appreciating its potential impact on the housing market.

To begin, let's dissect the concept of co-living. Picture a residence where individuals rent private bedrooms but share common areas such as kitchens, dining areas, bathrooms, and sometimes outdoor spaces. This design maximizes the use of space and reduces individual living costs. Unlike traditional rental properties where tenants have separate units, co-living spaces combine an environment of shared living and personal privacy. One might think that co-living is simply a modern term for having roommates, but the distinction lies in these spaces' intentional design and management. Traditional roommate arrangements often come together by chance, resulting in a mix of personalities and living habits that may or may not gel well.

On the other hand, co-living is a structured approach where the property's design, layout, and management are all geared toward creating a cohesive and harmonious living experience. Co-living redefines the traditional rental model by emphasizing access and affordability. Unlike conventional apartments, where the entire financial burden falls on individual tenants, co-living spaces distribute costs across all residents. This approach allows tenants to enjoy private spaces while sharing common areas like kitchens, lounges, and co-working spaces, significantly reducing overall living expenses. With utilities and maintenance included, co-living makes quality housing more accessible, enabling residents to live in desirable locations without breaking the bank.

Another critical difference between co-living spaces and traditional rental properties is how they are managed. In traditional rentals, property management often focuses on maintaining the property and handling issues as they arise.

From an investment perspective, the appeal of co-living lies in its ability to meet the changing demands of today's renters. Imagine living in a cramped apartment, juggling rent, utilities, and loneliness, versus a co-living space where you have your own private room but share beautifully designed common areas and expenses with others. For renters, especially Millennials and Gen Z, co-living offers affordability, flexibility, and a touch of style that traditional rentals often lack. For investors, it's a chance to cater to this evolving demand, tapping into a market eager for housing that fits both their budgets and lifestyles.

◆◆◆

A Co-Living Avatar

Meet Patty, a 28-year-old graphic designer who recently moved to the city for a new job. In a traditional rental, she finds herself in a tiny studio apartment. The rent consumes a large chunk of her paycheck, leaving little room for savings. She's also paying for utilities, internet, and a gym membership—all adding up quickly. Despite living in a bustling city, Patty feels isolated; her neighbors are strangers, and socializing requires going out and spending more money.

Now, imagine Patty in a co-living space. She has her own furnished bedroom but shares a spacious, modern kitchen and dining room with five other professionals. Her rent covers all utilities, high-speed internet, and even cleaning services for the communal areas. There's an on-site shared workspace, which means no more extra trips to Starbucks, and regular house events, like movie nights and Sunday dinners, make it easy to meet people. Patty not only saves money but also gains a built-in social network, making her transition to city life smoother and more enjoyable.

For Patty, co-living pros are clear: lower costs, fewer responsibilities, and a vibrant community. In contrast, her traditional rental setup was more expensive and isolated, and she lacked the added perks that make life easier and more connected.

◆ ◆ ◆

Co-living provides a solution to the affordability crisis by allowing for shared costs. In a typical rental arrangement, the cost of living is borne entirely by one individual or household. However, the expenses are distributed among multiple tenants in a co-living arrangement. This cost-sharing can make living in desirable locations more affordable, as the overall rent is lower than traditional apartments or single-family homes. For investors, this means the potential to offer competitive pricing while still achieving solid returns on investment.

Another thing that sets co-living arrangements apart from traditional rentals is their flexibility. Many co-living spaces offer short-term leases, which appeal to individuals temporarily in a city for work or study. Additionally, co-living spaces often include utilities, Wi-Fi, and other amenities in the rent, reducing the hassle and unpredictability of managing these costs separately. This convenience and flexibility make co-living an attractive option for a diverse range of tenants, from young professionals to students and digital nomads.

The Current State of the Affordable Housing Market

Affordable housing has emerged as one of the most pressing issues in the real estate market today. Rising rent prices and a growing affordability gap require innovative solutions. Understanding the current state of the affordable housing market is essential for anyone looking to make a meaningful impact, especially as an investor. Let's explore the market's complexities and challenges and see why co-living can be transformative.

The affordable housing crisis is not new, but its urgency has intensified recently. Across the United States, the disparity between wages and housing costs has reached alarming levels. According to various reports, many American renters are burdened by housing costs that consume a disproportionate share of their income. In major cities like New York, San Francisco, and Los Angeles, high rent prices have become a barrier to housing stability for many individuals and families. This imbalance is exacerbated by stagnant wages, making it increasingly difficult for people to find homes they can afford.

You might wonder, "How did we get here?" The roots of the affordable housing crisis are complex and multifaceted. On the one hand, there's the issue of supply and demand. Over the past few decades, there has been a notable shortage of new affordable housing developments, partly due to zoning laws, high construction costs, and regulatory hurdles. On the other hand, the demand for affordable housing continues to rise as the population grows and urban areas become more densely populated. This mismatch between supply and demand has increased rental prices, placing a heavy financial burden on many renters.

The problem is not confined to large urban centers. While major cities often receive the most attention, affordable housing issues affect smaller towns and suburban areas. As people move away from high-cost urban centers in search of more affordable living options, they are often met with limited availability and high competition for affordable units. This broadens the scope of the crisis, making it a nationwide issue that requires comprehensive solutions.

Co-living presents a promising solution to the affordable housing crisis in this challenging landscape. By leveraging shared living arrangements, co-living can address the housing market's supply and affordability issues. Let's delve into how co-living fits into this picture and why it's gaining traction as an innovative approach to affordable housing.

One of the primary advantages of co-living is its ability to reduce housing costs through shared expenses. Traditional rental properties often involve higher costs per individual, as each tenant is responsible for their unit. In contrast, co-living spaces distribute housing costs across multiple residents, leading to lower per-person rent. This model makes living in high-demand areas more accessible and affordable, offering a viable option for individuals who might otherwise be priced out of these markets.

Co-living helps address the affordable housing shortage by maximizing the efficient use of existing space. Instead of building new, expensive units, co-living can transform existing properties into shared living spaces, optimizing the use of available real estate. This approach not only addresses affordability but also helps to alleviate the strain on new construction and development.

Co-living also aligns well with changing tenant preferences, as mentioned previously. Today's renters are not just looking for a place to live; they seek environments that offer community, flexibility, and convenience. Despite its potential, co-living is not without challenges. Implementing successful co-living spaces requires careful planning and management. Property owners and managers need to ensure that the design and layout of the space support communal living and that the property is maintained to high standards. These factors are crucial for co-living ventures' success and achieving long-term viability in the affordable housing market.

Successful Examples of Co-Living in the United States

Co-living has quickly evolved from a niche trend into a significant movement within the real estate industry, particularly in affordable housing. To truly grasp the potential of co-living as a solution to the housing crisis, it's helpful to look at some real-world examples of successful co-living ventures in the U.S. These examples not only illustrate the viability of the model but also highlight how co-living can transform urban living and offer new opportunities for investors.

PadSplit

The housing crisis in the United States is multifaceted, with affordability and availability at its core. Finding stable, affordable housing is a constant struggle for many low—to moderate-income individuals, particularly essential workers. Enter PadSplit, a co-living platform changing the game by transforming single-family homes and underutilized properties into efficient, multi-tenant residences. This innovative model provides a lifeline to those often overlooked by the traditional rental market.

PadSplit operates on a simple yet transformative principle: maximize the utility of existing housing stock. In a typical PadSplit property, private, furnished bedrooms are rented out while residents share common areas like kitchens and living rooms. This approach not only makes housing more affordable but also ensures efficient use of space, helping to address the growing demand for housing without the need for new construction.

Unlike traditional rentals that require large upfront deposits, long-term leases, and additional payments for utilities and internet, PadSplit simplifies the process with a single, all-inclusive weekly payment. For members, this means predictable expenses, no hidden fees, and a significantly lower barrier to entry. For example, the average PadSplit room costs $729 per month, which includes utilities, internet, and furnishings—far below the national average for a one-bedroom apartment.

PadSplit presents a unique investment opportunity for property owners. By converting common spaces into rentable rooms, landlords can more than double their net operating income compared to conventional single-family rentals. This increased income potential makes PadSplit properties attractive for real estate investors seeking profitability and social impact.

Additionally, PadSplit's model generates significant taxpayer savings. The company estimates it has saved over $5.5 billion in taxpayer dollars by offering affordable housing without relying on public subsidies, reducing the financial strain on government-funded housing programs.

PadSplit's greatest strength lies in its ability to serve its members—individuals who often face significant barriers in the housing market.

Traditional rentals can be prohibitively expensive for someone like Sarah, a young graphic designer moving to a new city with high deposits, long lease terms, and fluctuating utility costs. In contrast, PadSplit offers an affordable and flexible alternative. Sarah can move into a fully furnished room within 48 hours, with all expenses rolled into one predictable weekly payment.

This model also fosters a sense of community. Unlike the isolation of traditional apartment living, PadSplit's co-living setup encourages social interaction. Residents often form supportive networks, sharing meals, experiences, and advice. These connections can be invaluable, particularly for those in transitional phases of life.

Beyond affordability and flexibility, PadSplit addresses a more profound need for stability and connection. Its properties often house essential workers—teachers, healthcare aides, delivery drivers—whose work keeps cities running but whose incomes might not match the rising cost of living. By providing a stable, affordable home, PadSplit empowers these individuals to focus on their careers, families, and personal growth without the constant stress of housing insecurity.

PadSplit is more than just a housing solution; it's a movement that aligns the interests of property owners, residents, and communities. Repurposing existing housing stock addresses the dual challenges of affordability and availability sustainably. Its impact extends beyond individual properties, offering a scalable model that could help bridge the housing gap in urban and suburban areas nationwide.

As the housing crisis continues to evolve, innovative solutions like PadSplit will play a crucial role in shaping the future of affordable living. For those seeking both profit and purpose, investing in co-living through PadSplit represents a unique opportunity to make a meaningful difference—one room, one home, and one community at a time.

Common

Common is another name in the co-living industry. Common operates in several major cities, including New York, San Francisco, and Chicago. Common's approach to co-living is a testament to the model's effectiveness in addressing affordability and community needs.

Their properties feature beautifully designed, fully furnished apartments that focus on creating a sense of community among residents. Common offers flexible lease terms, all-inclusive rent that covers utilities and Wi-Fi, and a range of communal spaces such as lounges and kitchens. This setup not only makes living in expensive urban areas more accessible but also fosters a vibrant community atmosphere. Their properties often include organized events and social gatherings, encouraging residents to connect and engage with one another. This emphasis on community-building is a key factor in

Common's success, as it addresses the growing demand for affordability and a sense of belonging. The company's ability to attract and retain tenants through its thoughtfully designed spaces and supportive community environment is a model for other co-living ventures to follow.

Bungalow

Another notable example is Bungalow, a co-living platform that focuses on providing affordable and convenient housing solutions for young professionals. Founded in 2017, Bungalow operates in several cities across the U.S., including Los Angeles, San Francisco, and Austin. Bungalow's approach to co-living revolves around simplicity and inclusivity. They offer fully managed properties with flexible lease options and all-inclusive rent packages that cover utilities, internet, and cleaning services. This model particularly appeals to individuals who seek hassle-free living arrangements and value convenience.

Bungalow's success can be attributed to its focus on catering to the needs of a specific demographic: young professionals who often navigate the challenges of urban living and job transitions. By providing a straightforward and affordable living option, Bungalow addresses the barriers to entry that many young adults face in high-cost cities. The company's emphasis on creating comfortable, well-maintained homes and fostering a supportive community aligns with the growing preference for co-living among younger generations.

WeLive

WeLive, a subsidiary of WeWork, offers another compelling example of co-living innovation. Established in 2016, WeLive provides co-living spaces in New York City and Washington, D.C., focusing on blending modern design with community-oriented living. WeLive's properties feature a range of shared amenities, including gyms, lounges, and event spaces, designed to enhance the living experience for residents. The company's model emphasizes affordability and lifestyle, offering flexible leases and various living options to suit different needs and preferences.

WeLive's approach to co-living highlights the potential for co-living spaces to integrate seamlessly with broader lifestyle trends. The company's properties are designed to cater to individuals who value convenience, community, and access to high-quality amenities. Combining these elements, WeLive has created a living environment that appeals to diverse tenants, from young professionals to digital nomads. Their success underscores the potential for co-living to offer more than just affordable housing—it can also provide a desirable and enriching living experience.

The Guild

Another example is The Guild, a co-living and short-term rental company that operates in several cities, including Austin, Dallas, and Houston. The Guild's approach to co-living focuses on providing stylish, fully furnished apartments with a range of amenities designed for both short-term and long-term stays. The company's properties feature high-end finishes, modern design, and a range of communal spaces, creating a premium co-living experience for tenants.

The Guild's success indicates the growing demand for flexible living arrangements. By offering a blend of luxury and affordability, The Guild caters to individuals who seek a sophisticated living environment without the high price tag of traditional rental properties. The company's ability to attract a diverse clientele, including both short-term visitors and long-term residents, demonstrates the versatility and appeal of the co-living model.

For women entering the real estate space, these examples can help them understand the potential of co-living and the factors contributing to its success. Studying these successful ventures can give you valuable insights into creating effective and impactful co-living spaces. Consider what aspects of these models resonate with you and how you can apply similar principles to your investments.

These co-living models of success prove one thing: co-living is not just a trend—it's the future of affordable housing. And you, as a woman ready to make her mark in real estate, have the chance to be part of this revolution.

CHAPTER 2

IDENTIFYING INVESTMENT OPPORTUNITIES IN CO-LIVING PROPERTIES

"By strategically investing in initiatives that directly improve people's lives...we can create a ripple effect that positively impacts society as a whole, essentially 'lifting up everyone'."

— Melinda Gates

Spotting Potential Markets for Co-Living

Finding the right market is crucial in real estate, primarily when investing in co-living properties. You want to ensure your chosen location has current demand and growth potential. The first step is to broaden your horizons beyond the traditional urban centers that have historically been seen as the gold mines of real estate investment.

Instead, consider emerging urban areas and secondary cities that show signs of growth.

Places like Austin, Texas, and Nashville, Tennessee, are becoming increasingly popular among young professionals who seek affordability and a vibrant community. The influx of millennials and Gen Z workers in these cities is palpable, and many prioritize the flexible living arrangements offered by co-living spaces.

Looking for gentrifying neighborhoods where revitalization is on the horizon is essential. These areas may be transitioning from economically disadvantaged zones to trendy hotspots. New businesses, improved infrastructure, and rising property values make them ripe opportunities for co-living investments.

You can strategically invest in an area with significant appreciation potential by identifying transforming neighborhoods. A neighborhood that once seemed undesirable can quickly become the next sought-after locale, mainly if it attracts creative professionals and startups looking for affordable housing options.

Next, consider the proximity to tech hubs, innovation centers, and large warehouses. These locations are critical because they draw a high concentration of young workers who often prefer co-living arrangements. Cities like Seattle, WA, Atlanta, GA, and Raleigh, NC, are excellent examples of how tech industry growth has led to rising demand for innovative living solutions.

Remote work has further fueled this trend, making suburban areas surrounding these tech hubs increasingly appealing for co-living developments. The appeal of co-living is that it caters to the needs of those looking for flexibility and community, which is increasingly attractive in today's remote working environment.

Furthermore, explore international opportunities. The co-living concept has gained traction globally, especially in urban areas facing housing shortages. Countries in Asia and Europe, such as Singapore and the Netherlands, have seen a surge in demand for co-living due to their high population density and expensive real estate markets.

As you conduct your market research, consider regulations and economic trends in these regions. Investing internationally can diversify your portfolio and give you access to untapped markets with lower competition.

Data analytics should be a significant part of your search for potential markets. Utilizing online platforms that aggregate real estate data allows you to identify trends, rental prices, demographic shifts, and other critical indicators. Keep a close eye on cities where rental prices outpace wage growth.

This discrepancy often indicates that residents will soon seek more affordable housing solutions, creating a perfect environment for co-living spaces. You can make informed decisions about where to invest using data-driven insights rather than gut feelings alone.

Key Factors to Consider When Scouting for Affordable Properties

When scouting for properties suitable for co-living, you must think beyond just the purchase price. While affordability is necessary, the property's potential to thrive as a co-living space is what you should prioritize. To start, the location and accessibility of the property cannot be overstated. You've likely heard the phrase "location is everything" in real estate, which holds true, particularly for co-living spaces.

Prospective tenants often seek convenience and accessibility to public transportation, major roads, and nearby amenities like grocery stores, parks, and entertainment venues. You want to ensure that your property is situated where tenants can easily commute to work and enjoy local attractions, enhancing their overall living experience.

The next factor to consider is the condition of the property and the associated renovation costs. Older buildings can often be a great deal, but they might require significant renovations to meet modern standards and appeal to today's renters.

This means you must account for the costs of necessary upgrades, including plumbing and electrical work and cosmetic improvements like paint, flooring, and furnishings. Understanding the total investment required will help you gauge whether a seemingly cheap property is a good deal or a financial pitfall.

Equally important is to understand the legal and zoning considerations surrounding any property you want to acquire. Some areas may have stringent regulations regarding rental properties and the number of non-related occupants allowed in a shared living space. Familiarizing yourself with local zoning laws can save you a lot of headaches down the road.

Failure to comply with these regulations can result in significant fines or even the inability to operate your co-living space legally. So, take the time to research and consult with legal experts to ensure that your intended use of the property aligns with local laws.

Moreover, don't overlook the potential for investment incentives and financial assistance that local governments might offer. Many cities are keen to promote affordable housing solutions and may provide grants, tax breaks, or low-interest loans for real estate projects that contribute to this cause.

Exploring these opportunities can significantly reduce your upfront costs and improve your return on investment. Finding a property that qualifies for such programs boosts your financial viability and aligns your investment with social responsibility, making it a win-win scenario.

As you scout for properties, always consider the potential for an area's future appreciation. Are there development plans for new businesses, schools, or public transport improvements? An area currently undervalued but poised for growth can yield substantial returns in the coming years.

Watch local news and community forums for discussions about upcoming projects that might enhance the area's appeal. Understanding these dynamics will help you make educated guesses about how the market might evolve and where property values could go.

Demographic Analysis and Co-Living Demand

Understanding the demographics of your target market is vital for making informed decisions about where to invest in co-living properties. This analysis goes beyond merely looking at numbers; it's about grasping who your potential tenants are, what they want, and how you can meet their needs. The primary demographic for co-living often consists of younger individuals, particularly millennials and Gen Z, who are drawn to flexible and affordable housing options.

However, the trend is evolving, and older adults looking for community living arrangements are also interested in co-living. This shift means that your property must cater to a broader range of lifestyles, making it essential to understand these different age groups' unique needs and preferences.

Income levels are another crucial factor when analyzing demand for co-living spaces. Co-living can be a lifesaver for many residents in areas with high living costs and relatively low average incomes. People in these regions often seek cost-effective housing solutions that don't compromise quality or community.

You can identify these areas by comparing rental prices to the region's average wages. When the disparity is significant, it clearly shows a demand for affordable living arrangements like co-living, which can significantly influence your investment decisions.

Understanding employment trends is also vital for assessing co-living demand. Cities with growing job markets, especially in technology, education, and healthcare industries, tend to attract young professionals seeking innovative living solutions. As remote work continues gaining traction, a growing population of digital nomads and remote employees require flexible, short-term housing arrangements.

By focusing your investments in areas with these employment trends, you can tap into a market actively seeking co-living options.

Social trends and cultural factors are also significant when considering co-living demand. The cultural shift toward valuing experiences over material possessions has led many to choose co-living as a preferred lifestyle. This trend is particularly prevalent among younger generations, prioritizing community living and shared experiences.

Understanding these social dynamics allows you to tailor your marketing strategies and property design to resonate with your target demographic. Highlighting aspects of community living and opportunities for social interaction in your marketing materials may effectively attract potential tenants in a targeted demographic.

Population density and urbanization trends further amplify the need for co-living spaces. Co-living has become an increasingly practical solution for many individuals and families in densely populated urban centers where housing costs are skyrocketing. By targeting urban areas with high population density, you can tap into a market actively seeking affordable living arrangements.

Observing migration patterns can also inform your investment decisions. If certain cities are experiencing an influx of residents, it becomes crucial to understand the underlying reasons behind this migration.

Economic opportunities, lifestyle preferences, and even climate factors can drive individuals and families to relocate. For instance, cities that expand their job markets or enhance their cultural offerings will naturally attract new residents seeking employment and a vibrant community life.

When considering co-living investments, focus on urban areas experiencing rapid growth. These locations often witness increased demand for housing as newcomers settle in. Areas like Atlanta, Miami,

New York City, and San Francisco have spikes in co-living interest due to the high costs of traditional housing and the influx of professionals drawn to tech and creative industries.

Understanding generational dynamics in urban centers is critical to refining your investment strategy. Millennials and Gen Z renters seek more than just a place to live—they prioritize shared experiences, social interaction, and sustainability. To attract these tenants, focus on creating spaces that foster community, such as inviting communal areas and versatile workspaces. Additionally, incorporating eco-friendly features can resonate with their environmental values, enhancing the appeal of your co-living properties.

Another demographic trend to monitor is the increase in single-person households. This shift, driven by delayed marriage, higher divorce rates, and the choice to live independently, creates a substantial market for co-living spaces. Many individuals in this category seek affordable living options without the isolation that can come with traditional apartments.

Co-living can provide the perfect balance by offering private living quarters, shared amenities, and social opportunities. By understanding this trend, you can tailor your marketing and property offerings to meet the specific needs of single renters looking for connection and community.

Demographic changes can offer valuable insights into future housing demand, particularly with the aging population. As older adults increasingly seek environments that foster social interaction and support, co-living presents a unique opportunity. By designing properties that emphasize accessibility, community engagement, and access to health services, investors can tap into a growing yet often overlooked market segment.

Consider using comprehensive market research tools and analytics to effectively analyze demographics and co-living demand. Platforms that aggregate demographic data, housing trends, and economic indicators can provide valuable insights into the areas you're considering for investment.

Use resources like census data, economic reports, and local news to understand market dynamics. Engage with community leaders, local real estate investors' associations, and local businesses to gain first-hand insights into neighborhood trends and demands.

Finally, remember that effective marketing is crucial in attracting tenants to your co-living properties. A targeted marketing strategy that resonates with your identified demographic will significantly enhance your chances of success.

Utilize social media platforms to reach younger audiences and consider partnerships with local businesses to create community events that draw interest. Focus on building a brand that embodies the lifestyle and values of co-living, emphasizing community, affordability, and flexibility.

A thorough demographic analysis is essential for identifying and capitalizing on co-living demand. By understanding population density, urbanization trends, generational preferences, and emerging demographic shifts, you can position your investments strategically within the co-living market. Tailoring your properties to meet the needs of diverse renters enhances your investment potential and contributes to a more connected and thriving community.

◆ ◆ ◆

Finding the Right Property for PadSplit: A Step-by-Step Guide

Choosing the right property is critical to the success of your PadSplit investment. Only some houses or neighborhoods suit this model; finding the ideal property requires careful evaluation. Below is a comprehensive checklist to help you identify the best potential PadSplit properties.

1. Neighborhood Suitability

The neighborhood can make or break your PadSplit's success. Here's what to look for:

- ***Class B or C Neighborhoods***: These are working-class areas with a stable population, such as teachers, gig economy workers, and factory employees. They provide a solid tenant base.
- ***Safe Environment***: Safety is crucial, particularly for female residents. Ensure that the area feels secure for residents walking or parking at night.
- ***Avoid Class A Neighborhoods***. These areas may be less accommodating of shared housing models, increasing the risk of complaints and conflicts.
- ***Look for Cars on the Streets.*** This indicates that residents are familiar with shared living setups, facilitating tenant acceptance and community fit.

2. Property Type

Your property's structure and parking are essential to its suitability:

- ***Size***: Look for properties at least 1,500–1,700 square feet to accommodate multiple bedrooms.
- ***Parking Availability***: Properties should have street parking or room to add parking spots, with at least two driveway spaces.
- ***No HOA or Minimal HOA Restrictions***: HOAs with strict regulations can limit the number of tenants or parking options, so avoid properties with restrictive covenants.

3. Interior Layout

A flexible interior layout allows for optimal room configurations:

- **Convertible Spaces**: *Properties with living rooms, dining rooms, or garages that can be turned into bedrooms are ideal.*
- **Room Requirements**:
    - *At least two outlets.*
    - *A door and a window for egress.*
    - *Heating and air supply, either central air or a mini-split system.*
    - *Minimum size of 8x10.*
- **Number of Bathrooms**: *To maintain tenant comfort, a full bathroom should serve at most four bedrooms.*

4. Location Advantages

Location impacts tenant demand and property value:

- **Proximity to Workforce**: *Choose properties near large employment hubs like warehouses, factories, airports, or Amazon facilities.*
- **Public Transportation**: *While optional, properties near public transit can attract tenants who rely on it.*

5. Property Price and Potential

Your investment's profitability starts with the purchase price and property condition:

- ***Price Below $300,000***: The PadSplit model should target properties under this price point to remain profitable.
- ***Condition of Property***: Assess renovation needs carefully. Significant repairs can impact your ROI, so ensure the investment aligns with potential returns.

6. Zoning and Legal Considerations

Understanding the legal landscape is crucial for compliance and sustainability:

- ***Inspect for Code Violations***: Avoid properties flagged for issues like overcrowding or building code violations.
- ***Local Laws***: Verify that room-by-room rentals are permitted in your target area to avoid future legal complications.

7. Exit Strategy

A well-planned exit strategy provides flexibility:

- ***Appreciation Potential***: Consider whether the property is in a transitioning or appreciating area. This will affect long-term value and your ability to resell or refinance.

8. Community Relations

Good relationships with neighbors can smooth your operations:

- ***Minimize Disclosure***: *When renovating, avoid over-sharing details about your PadSplit model. This can help prevent unnecessary concerns or opposition from neighbors.*

Using this checklist, you can streamline your search for the perfect PadSplit property, ensuring profitability and tenant satisfaction. Following these guidelines will help you build a sustainable co-living business while contributing to affordable housing solutions.

◆ ◆ ◆

Considerations When Scouting for a Co-Living Property

Understanding local housing regulations is crucial when searching for a potential co-living property. These regulations establish the legal framework for operating a co-living space and ensure the property is safe, habitable, and compliant with local laws. Overlooking these requirements during your property search can lead to costly fines, delays, or even the inability to operate your co-living business legally.

Research Local Housing Regulations

Start by familiarizing yourself with the housing regulations in your target area. Every city or municipality has unique rental property requirements, particularly those intended for shared living arrangements. Regulations often address:

- **Occupancy Limits**: Understand how many individuals can legally occupy a unit based on size and zoning classification. Co-living properties often involve multiple tenants sharing common areas, so ensuring the property aligns with local limits is essential to avoid overcrowding violations.

- **Health and Safety Codes**: Investigate requirements for smoke detectors, carbon monoxide alarms, emergency exits, and sanitation standards. Properties not meeting these codes may require upgrades, which can impact your initial investment.

- **Permits and Licenses**: Determine what permits are necessary for your intended use. If you plan to make modifications, you may need a business license, rental license, or renovation permit.

Researching these regulations upfront lets you identify properties that align with your goals and avoid legal complications later.

Consider Zoning and Neighborhood Dynamics

Zoning laws determine how a property can legally be used. Confirm that the property is zoned for multi-tenant use or that you can apply for a variance if necessary. Properties zoned for single-family use may present challenges if local authorities restrict shared housing arrangements.

Engage Local Experts

Navigating local housing regulations can be complex. Consulting with a local real estate attorney, zoning official, or housing expert can provide clarity and help you avoid pitfalls. These professionals can review potential properties, guide you through permitting, and ensure compliance with local laws.

◆ ◆ ◆

How PadSplit's Membership Model Revolutionizes Co-Living Compliance

When PadSplit expanded into new markets, one challenge loomed: navigating outdated housing codes designed to limit unrelated individuals from living in the same residence. Many cities enforce these non-related multi-occupancy regulations to address concerns about overcrowding, safety, and neighborhood integrity despite other areas of their code already addressing these issues. For traditional landlords, these rules could mean hefty fines or even being forced to shut down operations.

But PadSplit had a solution: an innovative membership-based housing model that redefined tenant relationships and met legal requirements. Instead of renting rooms to tenants in the conventional sense, PadSplit designed a membership program that treats residents as members of a housing club, not as traditional leaseholders.

This membership is designed to address compliance with many local laws by positioning the living arrangement as a shared housing solution under a unified umbrella. Members pay weekly dues that include utilities, internet, and services, eliminating the need for individual leases. This innovative approach aligns with many city codes that govern shared housing while reducing administrative complexity for property owners.

For example, in a city with strict limits on unrelated individuals sharing a home, PadSplit worked closely with local officials to demonstrate how its membership model complied with the spirit of the law while helping the municipality update its laws applicable to co-living relationships. By creating a single agreement that covered the entire property rather than multiple individual leases, PadSplit argues it is not subject to non-related multi-occupancy violations.

This approach also benefits members, who enjoy greater flexibility and simplified living arrangements. Instead of traditional lease terms, members sign a straightforward agreement that outlines house rules, shared responsibilities, and membership expectations. This transparency fosters trust and accountability among residents while ensuring compliance with local codes.

PadSplit's model has not only helped property owners avoid costly legal issues but also set a new standard for operating co-living spaces responsibly. By prioritizing innovation and collaboration with local authorities, PadSplit has built a system that benefits everyone involved—from the property owner to the community.

◆ ◆ ◆

Proactive Compliance Saves Time and Money

Understanding housing regulations during the scouting phase saves you from expensive surprises down the road. By carefully evaluating each property's compliance, potential for renovation, and alignment with local laws, you can make informed decisions and lay a strong foundation for your co-living investment. With the proper preparation, you'll set yourself up for success in creating a safe, legally compliant, and thriving co-living space.

CHAPTER 3

FINANCING YOUR CO-LIVING INVESTMENT

"You get in life what you have the courage to ask for."
– Oprah Winfrey

Financing your co-living investment is an essential step that can determine the success or failure of your venture. In the evolving real estate landscape, where opportunities are abundant yet competition is fierce, understanding the financial tools and resources available is crucial.

Whether you're an experienced investor or just starting your journey, knowing the difference between traditional and alternative financing options is vital.

Traditional vs. Alternative Financing Options for Investors

Understanding the traditional financing landscape is critical, but I want to empower you to explore alternative financing options that provide a more inclusive approach.

Understanding Traditional Financing

Traditional financing usually involves securing a loan from a bank or financial institution. This method can be straightforward with a strong credit history and financial stability. However, the approval process can be cumbersome and often requires substantial documentation, including proof of income, tax returns, and a comprehensive business plan. Banks typically assess your creditworthiness through your credit score and financial history, which can sometimes work against women investors due to systemic biases.

Some banks have recognized the need for diversity in their lending practices in recent years. They have begun offering programs explicitly aimed at supporting women entrepreneurs and investors. Researching local banks and credit unions with initiatives focused on female investors can be beneficial.

They may offer more favorable terms and a more understanding approach to evaluating your application. Look for lenders that actively support women-led businesses and have a reputation for promoting gender equity in their lending practices.

Unlocking Growth with DSCR Loans: The Investor's Secret Weapon

For real estate investors, especially those diving into the co-living model, securing financing can be one of the biggest hurdles. Traditional loans demand stacks of paperwork—W-2s, tax returns, and an impeccable credit score. But what if your personal income is unpredictable or you've maxed out on conventional loans? Enter Debt Service Coverage Ratio (DSCR) loans, a game-changing tool that allows the property's income to speak for itself.

Unlike conventional loans that scrutinize your personal finances, DSCR loans shift the focus to the asset itself. Lenders want to know: *Can this property generate enough income to cover its debt?* That's where the Debt Service Coverage Ratio comes in.

At its core, DSCR measures the relationship between a property's net operating income (NOI) and its annual debt payments:

$$DSCR = \frac{Annual\ Net\ Operating\ Income}{Annual\ Debt\ Payments}$$

A DSCR of **1.0** means the property's income is just enough to pay the mortgage. Anything above that signals profitability, while a ratio below 1.0 raises red flags. This shift in focus makes DSCR loans a perfect fit for co-living properties, where the potential for higher rental income is baked into the business model.

The Power of Leveraging Co-Living Income

Imagine this: You find a property in a working-class neighborhood, close to major employment hubs. It's a 2,000-square-foot home with five potential bedrooms. Instead of renting it as a single unit for $2,000 a month, you implement the co-living model, renting out each room for $700. Suddenly, your property is generating $3,500 in monthly income.

With a DSCR loan, this high income boosts your DSCR, making lenders eager to approve your loan—even if your personal income wouldn't have qualified you under traditional financing. The property pays for itself, and then some, while you focus on finding the next cash-flowing opportunity.

Challenges to Consider

Of course, no financing tool is without its downsides. DSCR loans often come with slightly higher interest rates and larger down payment requirements—usually in the range of 20-30%. But for investors focused on cash flow and long-term growth, these trade-offs are often well worth it. The key is ensuring your co-living property is in a high-demand area where rental income can comfortably cover the debt and then some.

The Bottom Line

DSCR loans unlock opportunities that traditional financing simply can't. By focusing on the income potential of your co-living property, these loans allow you to scale faster, earn more, and protect your personal finances. For investors in the co-living space, DSCR loans are more than just a financing option—they're the secret weapon to building a sustainable, cash-flowing portfolio.

Exploring Creative Financing Options: Subject to the Existing Financing (SubTo)

For real estate investors, particularly those in the co-living space, creative financing strategies can be a game-changer. One such strategy is purchasing a property *subject to the existing financing*. This approach allows investors to take over a property's mortgage payments while keeping the original loan in place. For co-living investors looking to maximize cash flow, this can be an incredibly powerful tool.

What Is "Subject To" Financing?

In a "subject to" transaction, the buyer takes ownership of the property but leaves the seller's existing mortgage intact. The buyer agrees to make the mortgage payments, but the loan remains in the seller's name. Essentially, you're stepping into the seller's shoes and continuing to pay off their loan under the original terms.

The key phrase here is: *subject to the existing financing*. This means the property is being purchased "subject to" the terms of the current mortgage, which remains unchanged.

Why "Subject To" Works for Co-Living Investors

The co-living model thrives on maximizing cash flow, and "subject to" financing is perfectly aligned with this goal. Here's why:

1. **No Need for New Loan Approval:** One of the biggest hurdles in real estate investing is securing traditional financing. Banks typically require a lengthy approval process, high credit scores, and significant down payments. With "subject to" financing, there's no need to apply for a new loan. You simply take over the existing mortgage payments, which often have more favorable terms than what you'd get today. For co-living investors, this means you can quickly acquire properties without the delays and hassles of conventional lending.

2. **Low or No Down Payment:** In many cases, "subject to" deals can be structured with little to no money down. This is a huge advantage for co-living investors who want to reserve their cash for property improvements or building their portfolio. Every dollar saved upfront can be reinvested into converting common spaces into additional bedrooms or enhancing amenities to attract tenants.

3. **Instant Cash Flow from Favorable Terms:** Because you're inheriting the seller's loan, you may gain access to:

    *   **Lower interest rates**: Especially valuable if the original loan was locked in during a period of low rates.

- **Lower monthly payments**: This boosts your cash flow, a critical factor in the success of co-living properties.

By minimizing monthly debt obligations, you can pocket more of the rental income from each co-living tenant.

4. **Avoiding High Interest Rates in Today's Market:** In a rising interest rate environment, locking in a new mortgage can be costly. "Subject to" financing allows you to sidestep this entirely by keeping the seller's lower-rate loan. For co-living properties, where cash flow is king, this can significantly increase profitability.

5. **Flexibility for Sellers in Distress:** "Subject to" deals often work best with motivated sellers who are facing financial difficulties, such as:

- **Pre-foreclosure**: They want to avoid damaging their credit but can no longer afford the payments.
- **Relocation or divorce**: Life changes force them to sell quickly, making them open to creative solutions.

By offering to take over their mortgage, you provide a win-win: the seller avoids foreclosure or a lengthy sales process, and you acquire a property with favorable financing terms.

Additional Benefits for Co-Living Investors

1. **Streamlined Entry into High-Cost Markets:** In competitive markets where prices are steep, "subject to" financing allows co-living investors to enter with less capital. This enables you to secure properties that might otherwise be out of reach under traditional financing.

2. **Faster Path to Scalability:** With reduced upfront costs and no need for lengthy loan approvals, you can acquire multiple properties more quickly. This is especially beneficial in co-living, where economies of scale amplify your returns as you grow your portfolio.

3. **Preserving Personal Credit:** Since the loan remains in the seller's name, your personal credit profile isn't impacted. This leaves your borrowing capacity intact for future investments or emergency funding.

Key Considerations and Risks

While "subject to" financing offers numerous advantages, there are some risks to be aware of:

*   **Due-on-Sale Clause**: Most mortgages include a clause allowing the lender to demand full repayment if ownership

changes. While this risk is real, lenders rarely enforce it if payments remain current.

- **Seller's Credit Risk**: Because the mortgage remains in the seller's name, missed payments could harm their credit. Clear communication and a written agreement are crucial.

- **Legal and Ethical Concerns**: Work with an attorney to ensure the transaction is structured properly and that both parties understand their obligations.

For co-living investors, "subject to" financing is a highly effective strategy that aligns perfectly with the model's focus on maximizing cash flow and minimizing upfront costs. By leveraging existing financing, you can rapidly acquire properties, preserve your capital, and build a profitable co-living portfolio. When executed thoughtfully, "subject to" deals can unlock opportunities that would otherwise remain out of reach.

Power of Partnerships: Pooling Resources for Greater Success

In the world of real estate investing, success often hinges on collaboration. Forming strategic partnerships with other investors or real estate professionals can be a game-changing move, especially when navigating the complexities of co-living investments. Partnerships enable you to pool resources, share risks, and leverage diverse expertise to scale your portfolio faster and more effectively.

Why Partnerships Matter in Real Estate Investing

Real estate is a capital-intensive business, and building a successful portfolio often requires significant financial and operational resources. A partnership allows you to combine strengths with others, creating opportunities that may be out of reach as a solo investor.

Here are some key advantages of partnerships:

1. **Pooling Financial Resources:** One of the most immediate benefits of a partnership is the ability to pool funds. Whether it's for down payments, renovation costs, or operational expenses, having access to a larger pool of capital can:

   - Enable the purchase of higher-value properties.
   - Reduce the financial burden on each partner.
   - Open doors to financing opportunities that require substantial equity or liquidity.

   For co-living properties, where upfront renovation costs can be significant, this shared financial responsibility can make all the difference.

2. **Sharing Risks:** Investing always comes with risks—market fluctuations, unexpected repairs, or tenant issues. In a

partnership, these risks are distributed across all parties. This not only reduces the individual impact but also fosters a team-oriented approach to problem-solving. When challenges arise, you'll have multiple minds working together to find solutions.

3. **Access to Diverse Expertise:** Every investor brings a unique set of skills to the table. In a partnership, you can tap into areas of expertise you may lack, such as:

- **Financial acumen**: Some partners may have a deep understanding of financing strategies, such as DSCR loans or "subject to" deals.
- **Operational experience**: Others might excel in property management, tenant relations, or handling renovations.
- **Market knowledge**: A partner with local market insights can help identify high-potential neighborhoods and properties.

By leveraging each other's strengths, you can make more informed decisions and execute your investment strategy more effectively.

4. **Expanding Your Network:** A partnership often means gaining access to your partner's professional network, including:

- **Private lenders**: Expand your financing options with access to capital beyond traditional loans.

- **Contractors and service providers**: Reliable teams can streamline renovations and maintenance.
- **Real estate agents and brokers**: They can provide valuable market insights and off-market opportunities.

These expanded networks can accelerate your ability to find, finance, and manage profitable co-living properties.

5. **Increased Buying Power:** Partnerships can enhance your ability to scale quickly. With combined financial resources and expertise, you may qualify for larger, more lucrative properties or secure better terms from lenders. For co-living investors, this means acquiring multiple properties faster, increasing cash flow, and building a robust portfolio that generates consistent income.

Types of Partnerships in Real Estate

Not all partnerships are created equal, and the structure of your partnership will depend on your goals and resources. Here are a few common models:

- **Equity Partnerships**: Each partner contributes a share of the capital and equity, and profits are split accordingly.
- **Joint Ventures**: Partners collaborate on a specific project, sharing profits and risks for that venture only.

- **Active vs. Passive Partnerships**: In some partnerships, one partner may take an active role in managing the property while the other provides financial backing as a passive investor.

Key Considerations When Forming a Partnership

Before entering into a partnership, it's crucial to lay a solid foundation:

- **Clearly Define Roles and Responsibilities**: Who will handle property management, financing, or day-to-day operations?
- **Establish Terms in a Written Agreement**: Include details about profit sharing, decision-making processes, and exit strategies.
- **Align on Goals and Values**: Ensure all partners share the same vision for the investment to avoid conflicts down the line.

Strategic partnerships are an invaluable tool for real estate investors, particularly in the co-living space. By pooling resources, sharing risks, and tapping into diverse expertise, you can tackle larger projects, accelerate your growth, and maximize returns. The right partnership can not only boost your financial capacity but also provide the collaborative support you need to navigate the challenges of real estate investing.

Seller Financing: A Creative Path to Property Ownership

Seller financing, also known as owner financing, offers a unique opportunity for real estate investors to bypass traditional lenders and work directly with property sellers to finance a purchase. This arrangement can be particularly advantageous for co-living investors, providing greater flexibility in terms and potentially faster acquisition timelines.

What Is Seller Financing?

In a seller financing deal, the seller acts as the lender, allowing the buyer to make payments directly to them rather than securing a mortgage through a bank. The buyer and seller negotiate the loan terms, including the interest rate, repayment schedule, and down payment.

Once the terms are agreed upon, a legally binding contract outlines the details, protecting both parties throughout the loan's term.

Benefits of Seller Financing for Co-Living Investors

Seller financing can offer several advantages, especially when purchasing properties for co-living:

1. **Simplified and Faster Closing Process:** Traditional financing can be a lengthy and cumbersome process, involving credit checks, appraisals, and underwriting. Seller financing eliminates much of this red tape, allowing for a quicker and more straightforward closing process. This can be crucial when time is of the essence in securing a high-potential co-living property.

2. **Flexible Terms:** Because the terms are negotiated directly between buyer and seller, there's room for flexibility:

   - **Lower Down Payment:** Sellers may accept a smaller down payment than a bank would require, freeing up your capital for renovations or operational costs.

   - **Customized Payment Plans:** Payments can be structured in ways that suit your cash flow, such as interest-only payments for a period or balloon payments at the end of the term.

   - **Lower Interest Rates:** Depending on the seller's motivations, you might negotiate a more favorable interest rate than you'd get from a traditional lender.

3. **Easier Qualification:** For investors with less-than-perfect credit or those who have maxed out their borrowing capacity with traditional lenders, seller financing offers an alternative path:

- Sellers may be more lenient about credit history, focusing instead on the value of the property and your ability to make payments.

4. **Potential for Creative Deal Structuring:** Seller financing allows for innovative deal structures that can benefit both parties:

- **Partial Seller Financing**: Sometimes the seller may finance only a portion of the purchase price, allowing you to combine seller financing with other financing methods, such as a DSCR loan.
- **Lease-Purchase Options**: Some deals may include a lease-to-own arrangement, giving you time to build equity and transition into full ownership.

Benefits for Sellers

Seller financing isn't just advantageous for buyers; it can also benefit sellers by:

- Providing a steady income stream from interest payments.

- Allowing them to sell their property more quickly in a competitive or slow market.
- Potentially offering tax advantages by spreading out the capital gains over the life of the loan.

Key Considerations and Risks

While seller financing offers many benefits, it's important to proceed with caution and ensure the deal is set up for long-term success:

1. **Legal Protection:** Ensure that a solid legal agreement is in place, outlining all terms of the deal:

   - **Promissory Note**: Details the loan terms, including payment schedule, interest rate, and penalties for late payments.
   - **Deed of Trust or Mortgage**: Specifies what happens if the buyer defaults on the loan.

   Working with a real estate attorney is essential to protect both parties and ensure compliance with local laws.

2. **Due Diligence:** Just because a deal doesn't involve a traditional lender doesn't mean you should skip your homework:

   - **Property Value**: Conduct an appraisal to confirm the property's market value.
   - **Title Search**: Ensure there are no liens or encumbrances on the property.

3. **Negotiating Terms:** While flexibility is a major benefit of seller financing, it's crucial to negotiate terms that work for both parties:

- **Interest Rate**: Ensure the rate aligns with current market conditions.
- **Repayment Schedule**: Structure payments to fit your projected cash flow from the co-living property.
- **Balloon Payments**: Be prepared for any large lump sum payments that may come due at the end of the loan term.

Seller financing is a creative and flexible tool that can open new doors for co-living investors. By eliminating the need for traditional financing and offering customizable terms, it simplifies the buying process and enhances your ability to secure profitable properties. However, like any financing strategy, success lies in careful negotiation, thorough due diligence, and proper legal protections. When executed correctly, seller financing can be a win-win, propelling you toward your investment goals while providing value to the seller.

As you explore these creating financing options, remember that each method has advantages and disadvantages. Conduct thorough research to identify the option that aligns with your financial goals and risk tolerance.

Empowering Women Investors

Empowering yourself as a woman investor means understanding your worth and the value you bring to the real estate market. Surround yourself with a supportive network of mentors, peers, and professionals who can guide you through the financing process. Engage in local and online communities focused on women in real estate investing, where you can share experiences, learn from others, and find potential partners or investors.

How to Secure Loans and Attract Investors

Securing loans and attracting investors for your co-living project is a multi-faceted process that requires careful planning, preparation, and execution. You must present yourself as a credible and trustworthy borrower while effectively communicating your vision and potential for success. This section will outline practical steps to help you secure financing for your co-living investment.

Crafting a Solid Business Plan

Your business plan is the foundation of your investment strategy. It is a roadmap for your co-living project, outlining your goals, target market, competitive analysis, and financial projections. A well-thought-out business plan demonstrates your commitment and understanding of the co-living market, making it essential for attracting lenders and investors.

When creating your business plan, include the following key components:

1. **Executive Summary**: Begin with a concise summary of your project, highlighting its unique aspects and potential for success. This section should capture the reader's attention and motivate them to explore further.

2. **Market Analysis**: Provide a comprehensive analysis of the co-living market in your target area. Include demographic trends, competitive landscape, and market demand. Highlight the benefits of co-living and why your project is well-positioned to meet this demand.

3. **Marketing Strategy**: Outline your marketing and branding strategy to attract tenants. Discuss how you plan to differentiate your co-living property from competitors and your approach to community building.

4. **Financial Projections**: Present detailed financial projections, including revenue forecasts, operating expenses, and potential return on investment (ROI). Be realistic in your assumptions, and use data to support your projections. Lenders and investors want to see a clear path to profitability.

5. **Funding Requirements**: Clearly state how much funding you need and how you plan to allocate those funds. Be transparent about your financing strategy and whether you're seeking loans, investors, or a combination.

Once your business plan is complete, be prepared to revise and refine it based on feedback from mentors or advisors. A polished and professional business plan can significantly impact your ability to secure financing.

Building Relationships with Lenders and Investors

Networking plays a crucial role in attracting financing. Start by identifying potential lenders and investors who are interested in real estate or co-living properties. Attend industry events, seminars, and workshops to connect with individuals who can provide guidance, support, or funding.

Establishing relationships with local banks, credit unions, and private lenders can also be beneficial. Take the time to meet with loan officers to discuss your project and gather insights on their lending criteria. Building rapport can increase your chances of approval when you submit your loan application.

In addition to lenders, consider reaching out to potential investors who share your vision. Create a compelling pitch that communicates your project's value proposition. Prepare a concise presentation highlighting your market research, business plan, and financial projections. Be prepared to answer questions and address concerns that investors may have.

Utilizing Online Platforms

In today's digital age, online platforms provide unique opportunities for securing funding. Consider utilizing crowdfunding websites specifically focused on real estate, where you can present your co-living project to a wide audience of potential investors. Be sure to showcase your passion for the project and demonstrate its potential for success.

Social media can also be an effective tool for attracting investors. Use platforms like LinkedIn to connect with real estate professionals, potential partners, and investors. Share updates on your project, engage with industry content and participate in discussions that showcase your expertise and commitment.

Creating a Compelling Investment Proposition

When approaching lenders or investors, focus on creating a compelling investment proposition. Highlight the unique aspects of your co-living project and how it addresses market needs. Emphasize the community-oriented lifestyle that co-living offers and the financial benefits for both tenants and investors.

Consider offering incentives to attract investors, such as profit-sharing agreements or equity stakes in the project. Be transparent about potential risks and how you plan to mitigate them. Demonstrating a realistic understanding of challenges can build trust with potential investors.

Demonstrating Your Experience and Credibility

While you may be new to the co-living market, there are ways to enhance your credibility as an investor. Highlight any relevant experience you have in real estate, property management, or business development. If you need more direct experience, consider partnering with seasoned investors or professionals who can lend their expertise to your project.

In addition to showcasing experience, consider obtaining relevant certifications or training demonstrating your commitment to professional development. This can include property management, real estate investing, or community development courses. Such credentials can enhance your reputation and increase your confidence in managing a co-living investment.

Grants, Government Programs, and Incentives for Affordable Housing

Navigating the world of grants, government programs, and incentives can significantly impact your co-living investment's financial viability.

Various resources are available to support affordable housing initiatives, particularly for women investors making strides in real estate. In this section, I will explore the funding opportunities to help you finance your co-living project while contributing to affordable housing solutions.

Understanding Government Grants and Programs

Numerous government grants and programs promote affordable housing development. These resources aim to support both nonprofit and for-profit organizations committed to addressing housing shortages and improving community living standards. As a woman investor, understanding these opportunities can give you an advantage in financing your co-living project.

- **Community Development Block Grants (CDBG)**: Funded by the U.S. Department of Housing and Urban Development (HUD), CDBGs provide funding to local governments for community development projects. These grants can be used for various activities, including housing rehabilitation, infrastructure improvements, and economic development initiatives. Research whether your local government has available CDBG funds to support your co-living project.

- **Low-Income Housing Tax Credit (LIHTC)**: The LIHTC program incentivizes private developers to create affordable rental housing. It provides tax credits to property owners who commit to renting a percentage of units to low-income tenants. If your co-living project meets the criteria, you may be able to change this program and reduce your overall tax liability.

- **Federal Home Loan Bank (FHLB) Programs**: FHLB provides funding to local banks and credit unions that support affordable housing projects. Explore whether local institutions are involved in FHLB programs that can benefit your co-living investment. Some banks may offer favorable lending terms for projects that promote affordable housing.

- **State and Local Housing Programs**: Many states and municipalities offer housing assistance programs that can provide grants or low-interest loans to support affordable housing development. Research local housing authorities and state housing finance agencies for available programs and eligibility requirements.

Applying for Grants and Funding Opportunities

When applying for grants, thoroughly understand the application process and eligibility criteria. Gather all necessary documentation, such as project plans, financial statements, and letters of support from community organizations. Tailor your proposal to align with the goals of the funding organization and demonstrate how your co-living project addresses community needs.

Additionally, consider collaborating with local nonprofits or community organizations with experience securing grants. Partnering with established entities can strengthen your application and provide access to valuable resources and expertise.

Exploring Incentives for Affordable Housing Development

In addition to grants, various incentives exist to support affordable housing initiatives. These incentives can significantly reduce your financial burden while promoting your co-living project's success.

- **Property Tax Abatements**: Some local governments offer property tax abatements for developers who create affordable housing. These incentives can help lower operating costs and improve your project's profitability.
- **Zoning Incentives**: Many municipalities have zoning regulations that incentivize affordable housing development. These incentives can include density bonuses, expedited permitting processes, and reduced development fees. Familiarize yourself with local zoning laws to identify opportunities that align with your co-living project.

- **Access to Infrastructure Funding**: Infrastructure improvements can be costly, but various government programs offer funding for infrastructure development in support of affordable housing initiatives. Investigate whether your project is eligible for infrastructure funding, which can enhance the overall appeal of your co-living property.

- **Partnerships with Housing Authorities**: Partnerships with local housing authorities can provide access to additional resources and funding opportunities. Collaborate on initiatives that align with community development goals and explore how your co-living project can contribute to affordable housing solutions.

Financing your co-living investment requires a proactive approach and a thorough understanding of your options. By exploring traditional and alternative financing methods, securing loans, attracting investors, and utilizing grants and government programs, you can set the stage for a successful co-living project.

As you navigate this complex landscape, remember that resilience and determination are key. Each funding avenue you explore brings you closer to realizing your vision for a co-living community that fosters connection and enriches lives. You have the power to create a positive impact through your investment, and with the right financial strategy, you can turn your dreams into reality.

CHAPTER 4

THE PURCHASE PROCESS

"Before anything else, preparation is the key to success."
– Alexander Graham Bell

Preparation is key when purchasing a property suitable for co-living. This chapter will guide you through the step-by-step process of finding and acquiring a property that aligns with your vision for a thriving co-living community. I'll share insights on negotiating terms to secure the best deals and highlight the legal considerations you need to consider.

Step-by-Step Guide to Purchasing a Property Suitable for Co-Living

The journey of purchasing a property for co-living begins long before you sign on the dotted line. It involves careful planning, market research, and understanding what type of property best serves your target demographic. Here's a step-by-step guide to help you through this crucial phase.

Define Your Co-Living Concept

Before diving into property searches, take the time to define your co-living concept. Different demographics will have different needs, and understanding your target audience will guide your property search. Consider factors such as location, amenities, and design features that will appeal to your desired residents. For example, a property geared toward students may require proximity to public transport and universities, while a community for young professionals might benefit from nearby nightlife and office spaces.

Understanding Market Demand for Co-Living Spaces

Once you've established your concept, conduct thorough market research. Analyze the co-living landscape in your chosen area. What properties currently exist, and what are their occupancy rates? Identify trends and preferences among potential residents. Online platforms and local real estate agencies can provide valuable data on rental prices, vacancy rates, and popular neighborhoods. By understanding the market, you can better position your property to meet demand and differentiate it from existing options.

Tools and Resources for Effective Market Research

PadSplit Market Analysis Tools

For those targeting affordable co-living spaces, PadSplit offers an excellent case study. Their market analysis tools provide guidance on:

- What income groups are underserved in specific areas.
- Ideal property configurations for maximizing profit.
- Case studies on similar properties' success stories.

How to Use It:

Leverage PadSplit data to identify gaps in your market and configure your property to fill those needs.

Furnished Finder Stats Tool

Furnished Finder provides data on mid-term rentals tailored for traveling professionals, such as nurses and corporate workers. With their Stats Tool, you can access location-specific metrics, including:

- Demand levels for furnished room rentals.
- Median rent prices in various neighborhoods.

- Demographics of rental seekers (e.g., occupation, length of stay).

How to Use It:

Enter your desired location to discover key insights into rental performance and demand. Use this to identify high-demand areas and determine pricing strategies.

Airbnb Rooms for Rent Analysis

Airbnb offers a wealth of market data for short-term and long-term stays. By analyzing the "Rooms for Rent" section, you can gain insights into:

- Pricing trends based on location and amenities.
- Customer reviews highlighting preferences and complaints.
- Seasonal fluctuations in booking rates.

How to Use It:

Search your target location and filter by room type (private, shared, entire place). Take note of average prices, occupancy rates, and popular amenities like Wi-Fi, workspaces, and kitchens.

Zillow Rental Manager and HotPads

These tools offer in-depth rental market insights by aggregating data from listed rental properties.

- Zillow Rental Manager provides average rental prices, vacancy rates, and property features that tenants prioritize.
- HotPads allows for heat maps showcasing rental demand and price comparisons across neighborhoods.

How to Use Them:

Analyze listings in your prospective market and compare them to your co-living model. Determine which amenities are standard in your area and where you can differentiate.

Mashvisor

Mashvisor specializes in helping real estate investors assess properties for both traditional and short-term rental opportunities. Key insights include:

- Cash-on-cash return estimates for various property types.
- Neighborhood-level analytics on occupancy rates and rental demand.
- Property comparison tools to evaluate profitability.

How to Use It:

Input your prospective property address to compare its potential as a co-living space versus other rental models.

U.S. Census Bureau & Local Economic Development Data

Understanding demographic and economic factors is crucial for targeting the right audience.

Tools:

- U.S. Census QuickFacts (Link)
- Local Chamber of Commerce Reports
- Economic Development Authority Dashboards

These sources provide vital statistics on population growth, median income, housing costs, and employment trends—key indicators of co-living demand.

Facebook Groups & Online Forums

Social media platforms offer real-time, grassroots-level feedback from communities you aim to serve. Relevant groups include:

- Travel Nurses Housing (Facebook Group)
- Mid-Term Rentals & Digital Nomads Forums

- Reddit's r/Airbnb or r/RealEstate communities

How to Use Them:

Join discussions, post polls, and gather qualitative insights from users sharing their housing needs and experiences.

Practical Application: Building a Data-Driven Strategy

Once you've gathered market data, the next step is synthesizing it into actionable insights.

- Identify high-demand locations with limited supply of co-living spaces.
- Determine the ideal price point based on competitor analysis and audience willingness to pay.
- Design your co-living space to include in-demand amenities such as high-speed internet, private bathrooms, and communal kitchens.

Market research is the foundation of a successful co-living operation. By leveraging the right tools and platforms, you can not only maximize profitability but also create spaces that genuinely serve your target audience's needs.

Five Most Common Ways to Buy an Investment Property

Purchasing an investment property for co-living is a strategic move, and choosing the right acquisition method can greatly impact your success. Let's explore five primary ways to buy a co-living property, each with its unique advantages and challenges. Understanding these approaches will help you tailor your investment strategy to your financial goals and market conditions.

From a Wholesaler: A Fast Track to Discounted Properties

Wholesalers are the treasure hunters of the real estate world. They specialize in locating distressed properties, negotiating deals with sellers, and then assigning those contracts to investors for a fee. This method can be particularly appealing for co-living investors looking for undervalued properties with the potential for high returns.

Imagine you're scouting for a large single-family home with the potential to convert into a multi-unit co-living space. A wholesaler brings you a property at 30% below market value. You've got a deal with room to add value through renovations. However, these transactions typically move fast, often requiring you to pay cash or use hard money loans. Your due diligence window is tight, which means you need to act quickly but carefully.

◆◆◆

Suburban Success – Macarena's First PadSplit

In a bustling Atlanta suburb, Macarena saw a golden opportunity in a three-bedroom, two-bathroom property offered by a wholesaler for $200,000. With her strategic mindset and passion for affordable housing, she envisioned turning it into a profitable PadSplit.

Step 1: Acquisition with Private Money Loan

Macarena secured the $200,000 purchase with a Private Money Loan from an investor association. This allowed her to act quickly and focus her capital on maximizing the property's potential through renovations.

Step 2: Renovation and Optimization

With a $75,000 renovation budget, Macarena undertook a comprehensive transformation of the property:

- ***Expanded Layout:*** *She converted the home into a five-bedroom, 3.5-bathroom property, including a full garage conversion. The new layout optimized every square foot, providing ample living space for tenants.*

- **Modern Upgrades:** *Energy-efficient windows, a new HVAC system, and durable flooring were installed to improve the home's comfort and reduce long-term maintenance costs.*
- **Enhanced Amenities:** *The kitchen and bathrooms were modernized with low-maintenance, tenant-friendly fixtures. A half-bath was added to the garage-converted bedroom for added privacy.*

Renovations were completed in just three months, staying on schedule and within budget.

Step 3: *Cash-Out Refinance*

Following the renovations, the property was appraised at $380,000. Macarena refinanced at 70% of the ARV, securing $266,000. This refinance allowed her to:

- *Pay off the $200,000 Private Money Loan.*
- *Reimburse $66,000 of her renovation costs, leaving only $9,000 of her own capital invested in the project.*

Step 4: *Launching the PadSplit*

With the upgrades in place, Macarena partnered with PadSplit to manage and market the property. Thanks to its prime location and modern amenities, the rooms filled quickly.

The Financial Breakdown

- **Gross Monthly Rent:** *$5,400*

- ***Operating Expenses (mortgage, utilities, and management fees):*** *$3,600*
- ***Net Cash Flow:*** *$1,800/month*

Timeline: *5 Months to Profitability*

From purchase to full occupancy, the entire process took five months. The property became a stable, high-yield investment that generated consistent cash flow.

Key Takeaways:

1. ***Maximizing Space Adds Revenue:*** *The garage conversion increased the number of rentable rooms, boosting gross income.*
2. ***Strategic Financing Creates Flexibility:*** *Using a Private Money Loan enabled Macarena to act quickly and leverage a cash-out refinance to recover most of her investment.*
3. ***PadSplit Partnership Drives Occupancy:*** *Working with PadSplit ensured high occupancy rates and streamlined property management.*

This first successful PadSplit solidified Macarena's reputation as a savvy real estate investor and laid the foundation for future projects. It's now a highlight example she shares through her WomenWise Academy, inspiring other women to pursue similar paths.

◆ ◆ ◆

From the MLS: The Traditional Route

The MLS is where most real estate transactions happen. It is a platform where real estate agents list properties for sale, offering a wide selection of options. For co-living investors, the MLS can be a goldmine of opportunities, from duplexes and triplexes to large homes ready for conversion.

However, buying from the MLS often involves higher competition. Properties are visible to everyone, including other investors and traditional homebuyers, which can drive up prices. To stand out, you'll need a strong offer and perhaps a willingness to waive contingencies—although I advise caution with that strategy.

Pro Tip: Work closely with an agent who understands the local market and co-living dynamics. They can alert you to new listings immediately and help you craft competitive offers.

Subject to Existing Financing: Creative Problem Solving

A "Subject To" deal involves taking over the seller's existing mortgage payments while keeping the loan in their name. This method can be a lifeline for sellers facing financial hardship or foreclosure, and it allows investors to acquire properties with minimal upfront costs.

Picture this: A homeowner with a 3% interest rate is struggling to keep up with payments. Rather than lose the home to foreclosure, they agree to transfer ownership to you, and you continue making payments on their behalf. For you, it's an opportunity to secure a property with favorable financing terms, making it easier to cash flow as a co-living rental.

Legal Note: Be sure to consult with an attorney, as not all lenders allow subject-to deals. Violating loan terms could trigger a due-on-sale clause, requiring full loan repayment.

◆◆◆

Sub-To Success – Macarena's Lakefront PadSplit Plus

In the serene outskirts of Atlanta, Macarena uncovered an extraordinary investment opportunity: a sprawling three-story, 10-bedroom, 4-bathroom lakehouse with two kitchens. The property, located just 45 minutes from downtown, promised breathtaking lakefront views and strong rental potential. Even better, she could acquire it via a subject-to (Sub-To) deal, requiring only a $13,000 entry fee.

Step 1*: Acquisition via Sub-To*

The seller was motivated to walk away from the property, allowing Macarena to assume their existing mortgage. She structured the deal to pay just $13,000 upfront, covering back payments and closing costs. To fund this, she partnered with an equity investor who not only provided the entry fee but also contributed $65,000 for renovations, conversions, and furnishings.

Step 2: *Renovation and Property Conversion*

With $65,000 in capital, Macarena transformed the lakehouse into a high-end PadSplit Plus property:

- **Space Optimization:** *The existing 10-bedroom layout required minimal structural changes, but she added premium furnishings and modernized finishes.*
- **Kitchen Upgrades:** *Both kitchens were remodeled to include stainless steel appliances, durable countertops, and ample cabinet space to accommodate co-living tenants.*
- **Bathroom Renovations:** *The four bathrooms were updated with sleek, modern fixtures and water-efficient amenities.*
- **Common Areas and Furnishings:** *Comfortable and stylish common areas were created, featuring high-quality furniture, shared workspace, and entertainment zones.*
- **Curb Appeal Enhancements:** *The exterior was spruced up with fresh landscaping and a new deck overlooking the lake, adding value and aesthetic appeal.*

Renovations were completed within four months, transforming the property into a top-tier co-living space.

Step 3: *Launching the PadSplit Plus Property*

With its premium lakefront location and high-end amenities, the property was marketed as a PadSplit Plus—offering not just affordable housing but a lifestyle. Within weeks of listing, the property achieved full occupancy.

The Financial Breakdown

- ***Gross Monthly Rent:*** *$9,500*
- ***Operating Expenses (mortgage, utilities, and management fees):*** *$6,000*
- ***Net Cash Flow:*** *$3,500/month*
- ***Equity Partner Agreement:*** *Net profits were split 50/50, giving both Macarena and her equity partner $1,750/month in passive income.*

Timeline: From Acquisition to Occupancy in 4 Months

From the day Macarena took possession of the lakehouse to full occupancy, the entire process was completed in just four months.

Key Takeaways:

1. ***Sub-To Strategy Minimizes Capital Requirements:*** *With only $13,000 as an entry fee, Macarena acquired a high-value property with minimal personal funds.*

2. ***Equity Partnerships Fuel Growth:*** *Partnering with an equity investor provided the capital necessary for renovations, allowing Macarena to scale quickly.*

3. ***PadSplit Plus for Premium Affordable Housing:*** *Offering a higher-end co-living experience with premium furnishings and lakefront views attracted tenants willing to pay slightly more for enhanced living conditions.*

4. ***High-Yield Potential:*** *The lakehouse not only provided affordable housing but also generated substantial cash flow, benefiting both Macarena and her partner.*

This successful Sub-To deal stands as a prime example of how creative financing and strategic partnerships can unlock incredible real estate opportunities. Macarena now uses this case study in her WomenWise Academy to teach others how to achieve similar success.

◆◆◆

Seller Financing: Building Trust and Flexibility

In seller financing, the seller becomes the lender. Instead of securing a traditional mortgage, you negotiate terms directly with the seller, such as the down payment, interest rate, and repayment schedule. This approach can be ideal for co-living investors who may not qualify for conventional loans or who want more flexible terms.

For instance, a retiring landlord might be willing to sell you their property and accept monthly payments over five years. This arrangement benefits both parties: you get the property without the usual hurdles of traditional financing, and the seller earns interest while offloading their property.

Key Consideration: Ensure the agreement is legally binding by working with a real estate attorney to draft the promissory note and deed of trust.

Equity Partner: Sharing the Risk and Reward

An equity partnership is a powerful way to scale your real estate investing business, especially when you have the expertise but lack sufficient capital. By bringing in an equity partner, you leverage their financial resources while offering your skills in acquisition, renovation, and property management. Together, you share the risks and, more importantly, the rewards.

How an Equity Partnership Works

An equity partner provides the bulk of the funds needed to purchase, renovate, and furnish a property. In return, they receive a share of the profits. This model allows you to focus on your strengths—finding deals, managing renovations, and overseeing property operations—while minimizing your personal financial risk.

Let's break this down with a concrete example:

Scenario: Joint Investment in a Co-Living Property

You identify a promising co-living property listed for $500,000 on the MLS. The total investment required, including the purchase price, renovations, and furnishings, is $200,000.

Roles and Contributions:

- Equity Partner:
    - Provides $150,000 (75% of the total investment) to cover:
        - $100,000 for the 20% down payment on a conventional loan.
        - $50,000 for renovations and furnishings.
    - Plays a passive role in the investment.
- You (Active Investor):
    - Contribute $50,000 (25% of the total investment).
    - Handle all operational aspects, including:
        - Finding and securing the property.
        - Obtaining a commercial loan (e.g., a Debt Service Coverage Ratio loan).
        - Coordinating renovations and furnishings.
        - Managing the property once it's operational.

Profit-Sharing Arrangements

Profits are typically split based on the initial investment percentages or another agreed-upon ratio. For this scenario:

- Gross Monthly Rent: $10,000
- Operating Expenses (mortgage, utilities, maintenance): $7,000
- Net Cash Flow: $3,000

If profits are split proportionally:

- Equity Partner (75%): $2,250/month.
- You (Active Investor) (25%): $750/month.

However, as the active investor, you may negotiate a larger share of the profits to compensate for your management efforts, such as a 60/40 split in favor of the partner, or a 50/50 split regardless of the initial capital contributions.

Benefits of an Equity Partnership

1. Access to Capital:
   - The equity partner's financial contribution allows you to pursue deals that would otherwise be out of reach.

2. Risk Mitigation:

    o   Both parties share the financial risk, reducing the burden on any one individual.

3. Scalability:

    o   By leveraging your partner's capital, you can scale your portfolio faster, taking on multiple projects simultaneously.

4. Passive Income for the Partner:

    o   The equity partner enjoys steady returns without the hassle of day-to-day property management.

<u>Pro Tip</u>: Draft a Comprehensive Partnership Agreement

A well-drafted partnership agreement is essential to a successful equity partnership. This document should outline:

- Capital Contributions: Specify how much each partner is investing.
- Roles and Responsibilities: Detail who will handle what aspects of the project, such as securing financing, overseeing renovations, or managing tenants.
- Profit-Sharing: Define how profits (and losses) will be split, including provisions for refinancing or sale of the property.
- Exit Strategy: Outline what happens if one partner wants to exit the partnership or if the property is sold.

Clear communication and well-defined expectations are key to preventing misunderstandings and ensuring a smooth partnership.

Equity partnerships allow you to play to your strengths while leveraging the financial power of others. With the right partnership structure, you can build a successful real estate business, offering both premium and affordable housing, without being limited by your own capital.

How to Analyze a Good Deal and Go Under Contract

In real estate investing, finding the right property is only part of the journey. The real work begins when you analyze the deal to ensure it meets your investment goals and then take the necessary steps to go under contract. A well-informed investor uses this process to mitigate risks, identify opportunities, and maximize returns. This chapter explores the essential components of deal analysis, from appraisals to inspections, and provides real-world case studies to illustrate best practices.

Appraisals: Knowing the True Value of Your Investment

An appraisal is a crucial part of the property acquisition process. It determines the property's fair market value, helping you avoid overpaying. Lenders rely heavily on appraisals to decide how much they're willing to finance. But even if you're paying in cash or using creative financing, an appraisal offers invaluable insight.

Best Practices:

- Hire a certified appraiser familiar with the local market.
- Request an appraisal that includes comparable sales (comps) within the past six months.
- Use the appraisal to renegotiate if the property is valued below the agreed purchase price.

Example:

A co-living investor in Charlotte, North Carolina, found a four-bedroom property listed for $450,000. The appraisal came back at $420,000. Armed with this information, the investor negotiated a $30,000 price reduction, maintaining profitability while securing a property in a desirable location.

Insurance: Protecting Your Asset

Insurance protects you from unforeseen events like property damage, liability claims, and loss of income. For co-living properties, you may need specialized coverage to account for multiple tenants.

Key Coverages to Consider:

- Property Insurance: Covers structural damage.
- Liability Insurance: Protects against tenant or visitor injuries.
- Loss of Rental Income: Compensates for lost revenue due to covered damages.

Case Study:

An investor in Tampa purchased a six-bedroom co-living property. Two months later, a kitchen fire caused extensive damage, forcing tenants to vacate. Fortunately, the investor had loss of rental income insurance, which covered $15,000 in missed rent, ensuring they could continue mortgage payments while repairs were underway.

Due Diligence: Uncovering Hidden Risks

The due diligence phase is where you dig into the property's details to ensure there are no unpleasant surprises after purchase. This process includes reviewing title reports, zoning laws, permits, and local regulations.

Checklist for Due Diligence:

- Verify clear title ownership and check for liens.
- Confirm zoning allows for co-living or multi-family use.
- Review local rental regulations to ensure compliance.

Pro Tip: Work with a real estate attorney to review title and zoning documents to avoid potential legal pitfalls.

Inspections: The Eyes Wide Open Approach

Inspections are your opportunity to uncover issues that could impact the property's value or safety. A professional inspector will assess the structure, mechanical systems, and overall condition of the property.

Best Practices:

- Schedule inspections early in the due diligence period.
- Focus on major systems: roof, HVAC, plumbing, and electrical.
- Use inspection findings to renegotiate or request repairs.

♦♦♦

Turning a Potential Disaster into Opportunity in Denver

In the competitive Denver real estate market, an investor named Sarah was on the hunt for her next co-living project. After months of searching, she found what seemed to be a perfect fit: a five-bedroom home in a rapidly growing neighborhood. The property had spacious common areas, a large backyard, and a location close to public transit and local amenities, making it ideal for her target demographic of young professionals seeking affordable, community-oriented housing.

The Initial Excitement

The seller was motivated, and the asking price of $450,000 seemed reasonable given the market. Sarah quickly submitted an offer, which was accepted after a brief negotiation. However, knowing the importance of due diligence, Sarah scheduled a professional inspection as soon as the contract was signed.

The Inspection Reveal: Severe Foundation Issues

During the inspection, Sarah received news that could have derailed the entire deal: the property had severe foundation issues. Cracks in the walls, uneven flooring, and signs of water intrusion in the basement all pointed to a significant problem. The inspector estimated that repairing the foundation would cost at least $25,000, with the potential for additional costs if hidden damage was uncovered during repairs.

For many investors, this would be a deal-breaker. Foundation repairs are not only costly but can also cause delays in renovations and leasing, affecting cash flow. However, Sarah saw an opportunity.

Leveraging the Inspection Report

Armed with the detailed inspection report, Sarah approached the seller to renegotiate the terms of the deal. She highlighted the unexpected repair costs and the risks involved in taking on such a project. While the seller was initially resistant, Sarah emphasized that other buyers might walk away entirely, leaving the seller to disclose the foundation issue and potentially face a longer time on the market or a lower offer from another buyer.

To her advantage, Sarah was well-prepared and presented a clear, professional case. She proposed a $30,000 price reduction, slightly more than the repair estimate, to account for the inconvenience and potential additional costs.

Successful Negotiation: Securing a Better Deal

The seller, eager to close quickly and avoid the hassle of finding another buyer, agreed to the $30,000 reduction. The new purchase price was adjusted to $420,000. This reduction not only covered the estimated foundation repair costs but also provided Sarah with a $5,000 buffer for other improvements.

Strategic Repairs and Added Value

Post-closing, Sarah hired a reputable contractor to address the foundation issues. The repairs were completed within six weeks, slightly under budget at $24,000. With the extra funds, she updated the property's curb appeal by repainting the exterior and landscaping the front yard. These *improvements, combined with the resolved foundation issues, increased the property's market value significantly.*

Once the property was ready, Sarah implemented her co-living model. She rented out each bedroom for $850 per month, generating $4,250 in monthly rental income. After expenses, she was netting a strong positive cash flow.

Lessons Learned and Key Takeaways

Sarah's experience highlights the importance of thorough due diligence and the power of negotiation. By leveraging the inspection report, she turned a potential deal-breaker into an opportunity to secure a better price and improve the property's value.

Key Takeaways:

- *Due Diligence Saves Deals: Comprehensive inspections can uncover costly issues but also provide leverage for renegotiation.*
- *Negotiation is a Skill: Presenting a logical, fact-based argument can turn challenges into opportunities.*
- *Buffer Funds Are Crucial: Always aim for a price reduction that gives you room for unexpected costs.*
- *Value-Add Opportunities: Addressing major issues and making additional improvements can significantly boost property value and rental income.*

Sarah's success exemplifies how a proactive, solution-oriented approach can turn even the most daunting challenges into profitable ventures in real estate investing.

♦ ♦ ♦

Financing: Securing the Best Terms for Your Investment

Choosing the right financing can significantly impact your bottom line. Whether you're opting for traditional loans, hard money, or creative financing, it's essential to understand the terms and costs.

Steps to Secure Financing:

1. Compare loan options for interest rates, terms, and fees.
2. Work with lenders experienced in investment properties.
3. Prepare financial documents, including proof of income and investment plans.

Case Study: Leveraging Creative Financing

A co-living investor in Austin faced stiff competition for a triplex. Traditional financing wasn't closing fast enough, so they turned to a private lender offering a hard money loan. The higher interest rate was offset by their ability to close within 10 days, securing a property that cash-flowed immediately after minor renovations. Once stabilized, they refinanced into a lower-rate conventional mortgage, saving thousands in interest over the loan's term.

Going Under Contract: Locking in the Deal

After thorough analysis, the next step is formalizing the agreement. Going under contract involves signing a purchase agreement that outlines the terms of the deal.

Key Components of a Purchase Agreement:

- Purchase Price: Reflects the negotiated amount.
- Contingencies: Protects you if financing falls through or inspections reveal issues.
- Closing Date: Sets a timeline for completing the transaction.

Best Practices:

- Include contingencies for financing, inspections, and appraisal.
- Specify seller obligations, such as completing repairs before closing.
- Review the agreement with your attorney or agent to ensure all terms are clear.

◆◆◆

The Power of Contingencies in Phoenix

In the vibrant real estate market of Phoenix, an investor named Lisa was eager to expand her co-living portfolio. She discovered a promising duplex in an up-and-coming neighborhood, close to a major university and several tech company offices. With three bedrooms in each unit and spacious common areas, the property was a perfect fit for her co-living model, which catered to young professionals and graduate students seeking affordable, community-focused housing.

The Offer and Contingencies

The seller was asking $425,000. After some negotiation, Lisa's offer of $410,000 was accepted. As an experienced investor, Lisa knew the importance of protecting herself with contingencies, especially when purchasing older properties. She ensured her contract included an inspection contingency, giving her the flexibility to renegotiate or walk away if significant issues were uncovered during the inspection.

The Inspection: A Major Setback

When the inspection day arrived, Lisa joined the inspector to walk through the property. Everything seemed promising at first—solid structure, no signs of water damage—but then the inspector made a critical discovery. The duplex was outfitted with outdated knob-and-tube wiring, a type of electrical system known for being a fire hazard and failing to meet modern safety standards.

The inspector explained that not only was this a serious safety concern, but it could also make securing adequate insurance difficult. The estimated cost to replace the entire electrical system was $12,000, a significant unplanned expense that could derail Lisa's budget.

Decision Time: Walk Away or Renegotiate?

Lisa faced a tough decision. The safety risk was non-negotiable, but the property still held immense potential. Thanks to the inspection contingency, she had options. Rather than walk away from a promising investment, Lisa decided to use the inspection findings as leverage to renegotiate the deal.

Negotiating the Seller Credit

Lisa approached the seller with the inspection report in hand, clearly outlining the electrical issues and the associated risks. She explained that while she was still interested in the property, the cost of repairs would need to be addressed to move forward. Lisa proposed a $12,000 seller credit, effectively reducing the purchase price to $398,000.

The seller, eager to close the deal quickly and avoid putting the property back on the market, agreed to Lisa's request after some negotiation. The new terms allowed Lisa to close the deal without compromising her budget.

Post-Closing Repairs and Improvements

After closing, Lisa immediately hired a licensed electrician to rewire the entire property. The work was completed in three weeks and came in slightly under budget at $11,000. With the remaining $1,000, Lisa upgraded the lighting fixtures, giving the units a modern touch that appealed to her target tenants.

A Successful Co-Living Launch

Once the electrical work was completed, Lisa furnished the units and began marketing them as co-living spaces. Within a month, all six bedrooms were rented out at $800 per room, generating $4,800 in monthly rental income. After covering expenses, including property management and maintenance, Lisa was netting $1,200 in positive cash flow each month.

Additionally, the updated electrical system allowed Lisa to secure comprehensive property insurance at a competitive rate, providing long-term protection for her investment.

Lessons Learned and Key Takeaways

Lisa's story highlights the importance of contingencies and strategic negotiation in real estate investing. Here are the key takeaways from her experience:

1. *Inspection Contingencies Are Essential*
    The inspection contingency gave Lisa the flexibility to address a major issue without risking her investment. This safeguard ensured she could either renegotiate the deal or walk away if necessary.
2. *Use Inspection Reports as a Negotiation Tool*
    The detailed inspection report empowered Lisa to negotiate a $12,000 seller credit. By presenting clear evidence of the issue and its repair cost, she secured a better deal while keeping the transaction on track.
3. *Prioritize Safety and Long-Term Viability*
    Replacing the outdated wiring not only improved tenant safety but also boosted the property's marketability and value. These upgrades ensured the property would remain a reliable income source for years to come.
4. *Contingencies Provide Critical Flexibility*
    Whether renegotiating or walking away, contingencies allow investors to adapt to unexpected challenges. Lisa's ability to pivot and renegotiate turned a potentially deal-breaking problem into an opportunity.

The Strength of a Well-Structured Deal

By leveraging the inspection contingency, Lisa protected her investment and secured a profitable co-living property. Her proactive approach and negotiation skills turned a significant obstacle into a stepping stone for success.

◆ ◆ ◆

Building a Strong Foundation for Success

Analyzing a property and navigating the contract process require diligence, expertise, and attention to detail. By mastering appraisals, insurance, inspections, and financing, you can confidently move forward with your co-living investment, knowing you've mitigated risks and positioned yourself for success. Real-world examples demonstrate that preparation and negotiation are key to unlocking the full potential of any deal.

CHAPTER 5

RENOVATING YOUR PROPERTY FOR CO-LIVING

"We delight in the beauty of the butterfly, but rarely admit
the changes it has gone through to achieve that beauty."
— *Maya Angelou*

Renovating your property for a co-living setup is a critical step toward maximizing your rental income and creating a space that attracts long-term residents. This process involves more than just a fresh coat of paint or minor touch-ups; it's about transforming your property into a community-friendly environment where people can live comfortably and productively.

You and I know that managing a renovation project can be overwhelming, but with the right strategies, you can navigate this journey efficiently. Let's explore what it takes to renovate your property into a thriving co-living space.

Renovation Strategies That Maximize Rental Income

When renovating a property and intending to turn it into a co-living space, every decision you make should be geared towards maximizing rental income while ensuring the space remains functional, comfortable, and attractive to potential residents. The key is to create an environment that offers value to your residents while optimizing the use of space to increase your return on investment. Let's dive into some effective renovation strategies that can help you achieve just that.

In my co-living properties, I use the PadSplit model to maximize the square footage of single-family homes by converting underutilized spaces into additional bedrooms. In traditional homes, areas like standalone dining rooms, oversized living rooms, and even garages often serve limited purposes or go unused. By reimagining these spaces as private bedrooms, I can increase both functionality and profitability, creating more rentable units within each property and making the home more efficient for co-living. This approach has been central to my success across most of my portfolio. With careful attention to design and adherence to local zoning and safety regulations, I ensure that each conversion meets tenant needs while maximizing rental income and enhancing the co-living experience.

Understanding the Needs of Your Target Market

Before you begin any renovation, you need to have a clear understanding of who your target tenants are. Are they young professionals, students, or digital nomads? Knowing your audience will help you make informed decisions about design, amenities, and layout. For example, if you're targeting young professionals, focus on creating stylish and modern living spaces that offer plenty of work-from-home options.

Focus on High-Quality, Low-Maintenance Materials

Renovating a co-living space requires a strategic balance between initial investment and long-term savings. While it might be tempting to cut costs upfront, opting for high-quality, durable, and low-maintenance materials ultimately pays off by reducing future repair and replacement expenses. In a shared living environment, where multiple tenants cycle through the space, materials must be resilient to heavy use and easy to maintain.

Flooring: Durable and Cost-Effective Choices

The flooring in a co-living space will endure significant wear and tear. From dragging furniture to the daily footsteps of multiple tenants, the material must be tough enough to handle it all without showing signs of wear. Luxury vinyl plank (LVP) flooring is an excellent choice. It combines the look of hardwood with the resilience of vinyl, offering resistance to scratches, moisture, and stains. Additionally, LVP is easy to install and replace in sections, making it ideal for managing localized damage without overhauling an entire room.

Kitchen Surfaces: Practical and Resilient

Kitchens are the heart of any co-living property and, as such, are subject to high levels of activity. Countertops should be both functional and aesthetically pleasing. Quartz countertops are an exceptional option—they're non-porous, resistant to scratches and heat, and require minimal maintenance compared to materials like granite or marble. For cabinetry, consider solid wood or high-quality laminate with a durable finish to withstand frequent use and occasional spills.

Bathrooms: Built to Last

Bathrooms in co-living spaces are high-traffic zones that face constant exposure to moisture. Investing in porcelain or ceramic tiles for floors and walls ensures that these areas remain easy to clean and resistant to mold and mildew. In addition, fixtures such as toilets and faucets should be chosen for their water efficiency and reliability. Look for products with a strong track record of durability and low maintenance, like chrome or brushed nickel finishes, which resist water spots and corrosion.

Walls and Paint: Durable and Washable

Walls in common areas are prone to scuffs and marks, making the choice of paint critical. Opt for high-quality, washable paint with a satin or semi-gloss finish for easy cleaning. In high-touch areas, such as hallways or near light switches, consider adding a protective wall paneling or wainscoting to prevent visible wear.

Outdoor Spaces: Low-Maintenance Landscaping

If your property includes outdoor common areas, choose landscaping elements that require minimal upkeep. Hardscaping with pavers or concrete, combined with native or drought-resistant plants, creates a welcoming space without the constant need for watering, mowing, or reseeding. Synthetic turf can also be a practical alternative for green spaces in areas with water restrictions.

Maximizing Bedroom Space

In a co-living environment, the bedroom serves as more than just a sleeping area; it becomes a personal retreat where tenants can recharge and find privacy. Therefore, maximizing both the functionality and comfort of these spaces is essential. Thoughtfully designed bedrooms can significantly enhance the tenant experience, leading to higher satisfaction and retention. At the same time, optimizing the layout and features can help you maximize rental income by appealing to a wider range of tenants.

Multifunctional Furniture: The Key to Efficiency

Space-saving furniture is an invaluable asset in co-living properties, where every square foot counts. Consider incorporating the following multifunctional pieces:

- **Beds with Built-In Storage**: These beds feature drawers or compartments beneath the mattress, providing tenants with extra storage without taking up additional floor space. This is particularly valuable in smaller rooms where space for standalone dressers or wardrobes may be limited.
- **Modular Furniture**: Pieces like stackable chairs or nesting tables can be easily rearranged or stored as needed, giving tenants the flexibility to customize their space.

Optimize Storage Solutions

Ample storage is a top priority for most tenants. Even in compact bedrooms, strategic storage solutions can make a big difference:

- **Built-In Shelving**: Maximize vertical space by installing shelves or built-in cabinets. These provide storage without encroaching on floor space and can be used for books, décor, or personal items.

- **Closet Organization Systems**: Standard closets can be upgraded with organizers that include shelving, hanging rods at multiple heights, and compartments for shoes or accessories. These additions help tenants keep their belongings organized and make the most of the available space.

- **Over-the-Door Organizers**: These simple and inexpensive tools can be used for everything from shoes to toiletries, offering additional storage without requiring permanent alterations.

Design for Comfort and Privacy

While maximizing space is crucial, it's equally important to ensure that the bedrooms are comfortable and inviting. Attention to the following details can create a relaxing atmosphere:

- **Lighting**: Provide both ambient and task lighting. Bedside lamps or wall-mounted reading lights give tenants control over their environment, enhancing comfort and usability.

- **Soundproofing**: In a shared living arrangement, noise can be a concern. Investing in soundproofing measures, such as thick rugs, heavy curtains, or even acoustic panels, can improve tenant privacy and satisfaction.

- **Neutral Color Palettes**: Use soothing, neutral colors to create a calm and versatile backdrop. This makes the space feel larger and more adaptable to different tenant preferences.

Personalization and Flexibility

Allowing tenants some freedom to personalize their rooms can make them feel more at home. This could include providing options for removable wall decals, or small shelves they can install to display personal items. Flexibility in furniture arrangements also allows tenants to tailor the space to their needs.

By thoughtfully maximizing bedroom space, you can charge competitive rents while providing an attractive living environment. Tenants are often willing to pay a premium for well-designed, functional spaces that enhance their living experience. Additionally, efficient use of space allows you to accommodate more tenants without sacrificing comfort, boosting your overall rental income.

Shared Amenities and Communal Areas

Creating attractive and functional communal areas is a cornerstone of successful co-living properties. These spaces serve as hubs for interaction, convenience, and relaxation. To enhance the value of your property and elevate the tenant experience, it's crucial to design spaces that balance practicality with a warm, inviting aesthetic. Let's explore how to optimize specific communal areas, including kitchens, dining spaces, and outdoor areas like porches and decks.

Kitchens: The Heart of Communal Living

The kitchen is often the most frequented communal space in a co-living property. To ensure it meets the demands of multiple tenants, it should be designed for both efficiency and comfort.

1. **Multi-User Functionality**

    - **Ample Counter Space**: Install large countertops or multiple workstations so several tenants can prep meals simultaneously.

    - **Double Appliances**: If space and budget allow, consider adding a second refrigerator, oven, or dishwasher to accommodate the needs of multiple users.

    - **Dual Sinks**: These make it easier for tenants to clean up without getting in each other's way.

2. **Organized Storage Solutions**

- **Labeled Cabinets and Drawers**: Designate specific areas for shared and individual items to avoid confusion and clutter.
- **Open Shelving**: This keeps frequently used items, like mugs or plates, accessible while creating a sense of openness.
- **Pantry Space**: Include a spacious pantry with shelves that can be divided among tenants for storing dry goods and snacks.

3. **Aesthetic Touches:** Use a neutral color palette with warm accents to make the kitchen feel inviting. Pops of color in backsplash tiles, barstools, or even small appliances can add personality without overwhelming the space.

Dining Areas: A Place for Connection

The dining area is not just for meals; it's where tenants can gather to socialize, work, or host small events.

1. **Flexible Seating Arrangements**

- **Large Communal Table**: A sturdy, extendable dining table can accommodate both small and large groups.
- **Bench Seating**: Benches can seat more people in less space and can be tucked under the table when not in use.

2. **Multi-Purpose Use**

- **Built-In Storage**: Add a sideboard or buffet for storing communal items like dishware, board games, or cleaning supplies.
- **Secondary Workspace**: Provide outlets near the dining area to allow tenants to use laptops or charge devices, making the space functional for work or study sessions.

3. **Atmosphere and Décor:** Incorporate pendant lighting or a statement chandelier to define the dining area. Use warm wood tones or metal accents to create a cozy yet modern feel. Artwork or a large mirror can add visual interest and make the space feel larger.

Outdoor Extensions of Living Space

Outdoor areas are often overlooked, but they provide a crucial space for tenants to unwind and connect with nature.

1. **Comfortable Seating Options**

- **Weather-Resistant Furniture**: Include a mix of seating, such as chairs, benches, and even hammocks, to suit different preferences.
- **Communal Tables**: Outdoor dining tables encourage tenants to enjoy meals or work outside, weather permitting.

2. **Functional Additions**

- **Grill or Outdoor Kitchen**: These amenities turn the porch or deck into a multi-functional space for social gatherings and meal prep.
- **Fire Pit or Outdoor Heater**: These extend the usability of the space into cooler months, making it a year-round amenity.
- **Shade Structures**: Awnings, pergolas, or large umbrellas provide protection from the sun and light rain, enhancing comfort.

3. **Design and Landscaping:** Use natural tones and textures like wood, stone, or metal to blend seamlessly with the outdoor environment. Add planters with low-maintenance greenery to create a calming atmosphere. String lights or solar-powered lanterns provide soft, ambient lighting for evenings.

Creating a Welcoming Atmosphere

While functionality is crucial, the aesthetic of your communal spaces plays a significant role in tenant satisfaction. A well-designed co-living property should feel like home, offering warmth and comfort while remaining neutral enough to appeal to various tastes. Here's how to achieve this balance:

- **Neutral Base with Accent Colors**: Use warm neutral tones for walls and large furnishings, then incorporate pops of color through accessories like cushions, rugs, or art.
- **Durable, Stylish Materials**: Choose materials that can withstand wear and tear while maintaining their appeal. Think wood, metal, or concrete for furniture and flooring.
- **Personal Touches**: Incorporate community boards or display areas where tenants can post messages, event flyers, or personal artwork, fostering a sense of belonging.

The Benefits of Thoughtful Design

Thoughtfully designed communal spaces do more than meet tenants' functional needs—they create an environment where people want to live, connect, and thrive. By investing in shared amenities that are both practical and visually appealing, you can increase tenant satisfaction, encourage longer stays, and command higher rents, all while fostering a vibrant, community-oriented living experience.

Energy Efficiency Upgrades

Energy-efficient upgrades are a win-win: they reduce operating costs while appealing to eco-conscious and budget-minded tenants. By focusing on weatherproofing, energy-efficient lighting, and water-saving fixtures, you can make your co-living property more sustainable, comfortable, and cost-effective. Here's how each of these upgrades contributes to a more efficient and appealing property.

1. **Weatherproofing Windows and Doors:** Properly sealing your property against the elements is one of the most effective ways to reduce heating and cooling costs. Tenants appreciate a home that stays warm in the winter and cool in the summer without excessive utility bills.

Windows:

- **Double or Triple Glazing**: Replacing old single-pane windows with double or triple-glazed models significantly improves insulation. These windows reduce heat loss in winter and heat gain in summer, cutting down on the need for constant heating or air conditioning.
- **Low-E Coatings**: Windows with low-emissivity (Low-E) coatings reflect heat back into the room during winter and block heat from entering during summer. This maintains a more consistent indoor temperature year-round.
- **Weatherstripping and Caulking**: Sealing gaps around windows prevents drafts and reduces energy loss. This low-cost solution can have an immediate impact on utility bills.

Doors:

- **Insulated Exterior Doors**: Solid core or insulated doors help prevent heat transfer, keeping indoor temperatures stable.
- **Weatherstripping and Door Sweeps**: These additions prevent drafts and air leaks, ensuring that your heating and cooling efforts are not wasted.

2. **LED Lighting: Long-Lasting and Energy-Efficient:** Switching to LED lighting throughout your property is a simple yet impactful upgrade that offers immediate energy savings.

Benefits of LED Lighting:

- **Energy Savings**: LED bulbs use up to 75% less energy than incandescent or halogen bulbs, reducing electricity consumption significantly.
- **Longevity**: LEDs last 25,000 to 50,000 hours, meaning fewer replacements are needed—a crucial advantage in high-use areas like kitchens, hallways, and bathrooms.
- **Lower Heat Emission**: LEDs produce minimal heat, reducing the strain on cooling systems during warmer months.

Strategic Uses:

- **Common Areas**: Use LED ceiling fixtures and recessed lighting in kitchens, dining spaces, and hallways.
- **Task Lighting**: Install under-cabinet LED strips in the kitchen for improved visibility during food prep.
- **Outdoor Spaces**: Solar-powered LED lights for porches, decks, and pathways offer sustainability and security.

3. **Low-Flow Faucets and Showerheads:** Water efficiency is particularly important in co-living properties, where multiple tenants may use the kitchen and bathroom facilities frequently.

Low-Flow Faucets:

- **Water Savings**: Low-flow faucets can reduce water use by up to 30% without compromising water pressure, which tenants will appreciate in both kitchens and bathrooms.
- **Aerators**: Many modern low-flow faucets include aerators that mix air with water, maintaining a strong stream while using less water overall.

Low-Flow Showerheads:

- **High Efficiency**: These showerheads typically use 1.5 to 2.0 gallons per minute (GPM) compared to the standard 2.5 GPM, saving significant amounts of water over time.

- **Enhanced User Experience**: Many models offer adjustable spray patterns, providing a satisfying shower experience despite lower water usage.

4. **Low-Flow Toilets: Reducing Water Waste:** Toilets account for a large portion of household water usage. Upgrading to low-flow or dual-flush toilets is an essential step in making your property more efficient.

Low-Flow Toilets:

- **Water Efficiency**: Modern low-flow toilets use as little as 1.28 gallons per flush (GPF), compared to older models that can use 3.5 GPF or more.
- **Reduced Utility Bills**: With multiple tenants using the facilities daily, these savings quickly add up, benefiting both tenants and property owners.

Dual-Flush Toilets:

- **Customizable Flushing**: Tenants can choose a light flush (0.8-1.0 GPF) for liquid waste or a full flush for solid waste, optimizing water usage based on need.

Financial and Environmental Benefits of Energy Efficiency

1. **Lower Operating Costs:** Energy-efficient upgrades directly impact your bottom line by reducing utility bills. In co-living properties, where energy and water usage can be high due to multiple tenants, these savings can be substantial.

2. **Increased Tenant Satisfaction:** Budget-conscious tenants appreciate properties with lower utility costs. Moreover, eco-conscious renters actively seek out homes with sustainable features, making your property more competitive in the rental market.

3. **Positive Environmental Impact:** Energy-efficient lighting, weatherproofing, and water-saving fixtures contribute to a reduced carbon footprint. By implementing these upgrades, you're not only saving money but also supporting broader sustainability goals.

4. **Enhanced Property Value:** Energy-efficient properties are more attractive to buyers and investors. These upgrades can increase your property's market value, providing long-term financial benefits.

Smart Home Technology

Integrating smart home technology into your co-living property can be a game-changer. Features like smart locks and programmable thermostats that can be controlled through a smartphone app are Smart home features that also provide you, the landlord, with better control over the property, allowing you to monitor energy use and enhance security remotely.

Incorporate Stylish but Neutral Decor

While creating a visually appealing environment is essential, it's equally crucial to keep the decor relatively neutral. Bold colors and unique design choices might only appeal to a niche market, whereas neutral tones and classic design elements are more universally appealing. Consider it setting the stage for your tenants to add their personal touch to the space. By keeping the decor simple yet stylish, you open up the potential to attract a broader range of tenants who can easily envision the space as their own.

Safety and Security Upgrades

Safety should always be a priority when renovating any rental property, especially for a co-living setup. Install secure locks on all doors and consider a keyless entry system to simplify access. Security cameras in common areas can provide an extra layer of safety without invading your tenants' privacy. Ensuring your property is well-lit, inside and out, can also make residents feel more secure and comfortable. This attention to safety protects your tenants and adds to the property's overall value, making it more attractive to potential renters.

Final Touches and Finishing Details

The last step in your renovation should focus on the finishing touches that make a property feel like a home. Small details like stylish light fixtures, modern hardware, and tasteful wall art can make a big difference in how the space is perceived. You don't have to break the bank on these elements, but a well-thought-out design can significantly elevate your co-living space's overall look and feel, making it more inviting to prospective renters.

Evaluating the ROI of Your Renovation

After the renovation is complete, evaluating the return on investment (ROI) is crucial. Did your upgrades contribute to a higher rental income, reduced vacancy rates, or increased tenant satisfaction? Understanding the impact of your renovations helps you make informed decisions for future projects and ensures that every dollar you spent was put to good use. Keeping track of these metrics will guide you in fine-tuning your strategy to maximize your co-living property's potential.

Budgeting for Renovations and Ensuring Cost Efficiency

When renovating your property for co-living, budgeting is the foundation that can make or break your project. The importance of creating a solid financial plan cannot be overstated. Renovations can quickly spiral out of control if you don't have a clear budget, so let's focus on allocating your funds wisely to ensure maximum efficiency.

Setting a Realistic Budget

First things first, you need to set a realistic budget that aligns with your vision. Ask yourself, how much are you willing to spend on this renovation? While it's tempting to go all out, keeping your budget within your financial comfort zone is essential. To get started, list out all the elements of the renovation, from major expenses like structural changes to minor details like interior decor.

I recommend creating a spreadsheet that includes all the costs, down to the smallest details. This way, you'll have a clearer picture of where your money is going. Don't forget to include a buffer of around 10-20% of the total budget to cover any unexpected expenses that may arise during the renovation process. Surprises are inevitable, so it's best to prepare for them.

Prioritizing Essential Upgrades

Once you've set your budget, the next step is to prioritize. Only some changes you want to make will have the same impact on your co-living space, so you need to decide which upgrades are essential and which can wait. Focus on the elements that will directly enhance your residents' living experience. This might include adding additional bathrooms, improving kitchen facilities, or upgrading the common areas.

Furnishing and Finishing Your Co-Living Space

Creating a stylish, functional, and durable co-living environment doesn't have to break the bank. With strategic sourcing and a willingness to explore various options, you can furnish your property beautifully while staying within budget. By blending refurbished pieces with quality affordable items from platforms like Amazon, Wayfair, and The Minoan Experience, you can achieve a cohesive, high-end look for less.

1. **Refurbish and Reuse: Maximize What You Already Have:** Before jumping into new purchases, assess what's already available in the property. A little creativity and elbow grease can breathe new life into existing furniture and fixtures.

   Examples of Refurbishing:

- **Wood Furniture**: Sanding and staining an old dining table or set of chairs can transform them into statement pieces.

- **Cabinetry**: Instead of replacing kitchen cabinets, consider repainting or refacing them. Adding modern hardware can make them look brand new at a fraction of the cost.

- **Floors**: If hardwood floors are in decent condition, a professional cleaning, sanding, and polish can restore their original charm without the expense of replacement.

- **Lighting Fixtures**: Repainting or updating light fixtures with new shades or bulbs can modernize a room instantly.

2. **Affordable Furnishings from Trusted Retailers:** Balancing quality and affordability is key when furnishing a co-living property. The following retailers offer cost-effective solutions without sacrificing style or durability:

Amazon

- **Wide Variety**: Amazon offers everything from essentials to stylish statement pieces. Look for highly rated items with ample reviews.

- **Budget-Friendly Finds**: You can furnish kitchens and dining areas with affordable yet durable options like bar stools, dining tables, and shelving units.

- **Prime Perks**: Fast, often free shipping can be a lifesaver when outfitting multiple rooms on a tight timeline.

Wayfair

- **Curated Collections**: Wayfair provides a vast selection of affordable furniture and décor for all styles.
- **Bundles and Discounts**: Look for bundle deals on dining sets or bedroom furniture, which can save money while ensuring a cohesive look.
- **Room Visualizer**: Use their online tools to visualize how pieces will look together in a space.

The Minoan Experience

- **Wholesale Pricing**: This platform partners with leading brands to offer furnishings, housewares, and décor at discounted prices for property owners and managers.
- **High-Quality Brands**: Access to well-known, durable brands ensures your co-living property maintains a polished and professional aesthetic.
- **Streamlined Process**: Their concierge-style service simplifies the shopping experience, helping you outfit an entire property efficiently.

3. **Sourcing from Second-Hand and Discount Suppliers:**
    Sourcing second-hand or discounted items can uncover hidden
    gems and add character to your property.

Thrift Stores and Vintage Shops

- **Unique Finds**: Discover one-of-a-kind items, such as
  vintage dining sets or accent chairs, that add charm and
  personality.
- **Eco-Friendly**: Reusing items reduces waste, appealing to
  environmentally conscious tenants.

Furniture Outlets and Clearance Sections

- **Discounted New Items**: Many retailers offer steep
  discounts on showroom models, discontinued lines, or items
  with minor cosmetic flaws.

Facebook Marketplace and Local Classifieds

- **Affordable and Convenient**: Local sellers often offer gently
  used furniture and appliances at bargain prices. You might
  even find free items for pick-up.

4. **Prioritizing Value and Durability:** When furnishing a co-living
    property, durability is just as important as affordability. Frequent

use by multiple tenants means furnishings and fixtures must withstand wear and tear.

Tips for Prioritizing Durability:

- **Opt for Solid Materials**: Choose furniture made from solid wood, metal, or high-quality engineered materials that last longer than particle board.
- **Stain-Resistant Fabrics**: For upholstered items like dining chairs, opt for fabrics treated with stain-resistant finishes. Alternatively, consider slipcovers that are easy to clean or replace.
- **Multi-Functional Pieces**: Look for items like storage benches, extendable tables, or stackable chairs to maximize utility and save space.

5. **Creative DIY Solutions:** Adding a personal touch through DIY projects can enhance the property's aesthetic and save money.

Examples of DIY Projects:

- **Custom Shelving**: Build floating shelves using affordable wood planks and brackets from hardware stores.
- **Wall Art**: Frame inexpensive prints, posters, or even fabric to create a gallery wall.

- **Lighting Upgrades**: Customize pendant lights or lampshades with paint, fabric, or other materials to match your property's theme.

By combining refurbished items with quality yet affordable new pieces from trusted retailers, you can furnish your co-living property beautifully and cost-effectively. Explore second-hand stores, take advantage of wholesale platforms like The Minoan Experience, and embrace DIY creativity to add unique touches. These strategies will help you create a functional and appealing environment that tenants will love, all while keeping your budget in check.

Monitoring and Adjusting the Budget as Needed

Throughout the renovation process, it's crucial to continuously monitor your spending to ensure that you are staying on track. I suggest reviewing your budget weekly to see where you stand and if any adjustments are needed. If you're over budget in one area, look for ways to cut costs elsewhere. Remember, flexibility is vital when managing a renovation budget.

Don't hesitate to make difficult decisions if necessary. Sometimes, you may have to compromise on less critical elements to ensure that the most important aspects of the project are completed within budget. It's all about finding the right balance between cost and quality.

Finding a General Contractor for Co-Living Conversions

Renovating a property for co-living isn't your typical home makeover. It requires a contractor with specialized skills, experience, and a deep understanding of the unique demands of co-living spaces. The right General Contractor (GC) can take your vision and transform it into a profitable, functional, and welcoming co-living environment. However, hiring the wrong one can lead to financial losses, tenant dissatisfaction, and endless frustration. Here's how to find a great GC to ensure your project runs smoothly and successfully.

1. **Look for Experience in Co-Living or Multifamily Conversions:** Not all contractors are created equal, and co-living properties have unique challenges that set them apart from traditional renovations. When vetting potential GCs, prioritize those with specific experience in co-living or multifamily projects.

Why This Matters:

- Co-living spaces require a balance between private and communal areas. A GC with relevant experience will understand the importance of optimizing layouts for shared amenities like kitchens, bathrooms, and dining areas.

- Noise control, privacy, and durability are critical in co-living environments. Contractors who've worked on similar projects will know how to implement soundproofing, choose low-maintenance materials, and design for high traffic.

How to Verify:

- Ask for a portfolio of past projects, specifically highlighting co-living or multifamily conversions.
- Request references from clients with similar projects. Follow up by visiting completed properties if possible.

2. **Vet Their Credentials and Reputation:** The best GCs will have the proper licenses, insurance, and a solid track record of delivering high-quality work on time and within budget.

Key Steps to Vetting:

- **Check Licensing and Certifications**: Verify that the GC is licensed to work in your state or locality. Specialized certifications (e.g., for green building or energy efficiency) can also be a plus.

- **Confirm Insurance**: Ensure the contractor carries both liability and workers' compensation insurance. This protects you in case of accidents or damage during the project.

- **Research Their Reputation**: Look for reviews on platforms like Google, Yelp, or Houzz. Check the Better Business Bureau (BBB) for complaints or disputes.

Red Flags:

- Unwillingness to provide references or credentials.

- A history of poor reviews, particularly around communication, budget adherence, or project delays.

3. **Get Detailed Bids and Compare:** Once you've narrowed down your list of candidates, request detailed bids from at least three contractors. A comprehensive bid should include a breakdown of labor, materials, timelines, and costs.

What to Look For:

- **Transparency**: The bid should clearly outline what's included and any potential extras or contingencies.

- **Competitive Pricing**: Be cautious of bids that are significantly lower than others; this could be a sign of inexperience, cutting corners, or hidden costs.

- **Understanding of Scope**: A GC experienced in co-living conversions will ask the right questions about tenant needs, shared amenities, and durable finishes, demonstrating they understand the project requirements.

4. **Prioritize Communication and Project Management:** A great GC isn't just skilled with a hammer—they're also excellent communicators and project managers. Clear, consistent communication is crucial to ensuring your project stays on track.

Assess Communication During the Interview Process:

- Do they listen carefully to your goals and concerns?
- Are they proactive in suggesting solutions or improvements?
- How do they plan to keep you updated during the project?

Look for Strong Project Management Tools and Practices:

- A well-organized GC will use project management software or tools to track timelines, budgets, and daily progress.
- They should have a clear process for handling change orders, unexpected issues, and inspections.

5. **Start with a Trial Project or Small Task:** If you're hesitant to commit to a large-scale renovation right away, consider starting with a smaller project, such as a single room or a specific system upgrade (e.g., installing new plumbing for additional bathrooms).

This will give you a sense of their work quality, reliability, and how well they communicate.

6. **Build a Strong Contract:** Once you've selected your GC, formalize the agreement with a comprehensive contract. A detailed contract protects both parties and ensures expectations are clear.

Must-Have Elements in Your Contract:

- **Scope of Work**: Clear description of the work to be completed, including specific materials and brands to be used.
- **Timeline**: Project start and end dates, with milestones for key phases.
- **Payment Schedule**: Specify payment amounts tied to milestones, not time. Avoid paying large amounts upfront.
- **Warranties**: Include warranties for both labor and materials.
- **Contingency Plans**: Outline how unexpected issues will be handled and what happens if delays occur.

◆ ◆ ◆

A Tale of Two Contractors

The Bad Experience

An investor hired a general contractor without thoroughly vetting their experience in co-living conversions. The GC, skilled in single-family renovations but inexperienced in shared spaces, ignored critical needs like soundproofing and communal space optimization. This led to tenant complaints about noise and overcrowding, forcing the investor to spend additional time and money on fixes.

The Good Experience

After the setback, the investor hired a GC specializing in multifamily and co-living projects. This contractor optimized the layout, added soundproofing between walls, and installed durable, low-maintenance materials in high-traffic areas. They also provided regular updates, quickly addressed issues, and completed the project within budget and on schedule. The result was a well-designed property that tenants loved, leading to high occupancy and strong cash flow.

The Right GC Makes All the Difference

Renovating for co-living is a complex, specialized process, and the success of your project hinges on finding the right contractor. By thoroughly vetting candidates, prioritizing experience, and building a strong working relationship, you can avoid costly mistakes and transform your property into a thriving co-living space.

◆ ◆ ◆

Managing the Renovation Process

Once the renovation starts, your role shifts to project management. Even if you have the most reliable contractors, you need to keep a close eye on the progress to ensure everything is going according to plan. Regular site visits are a must; this allows you to address any issues or changes in real-time.

Communication is critical during this stage. Make it a point to have daily or weekly check-ins with your contractors to discuss the progress, potential delays, or adjustments that need to be made. You're not just the owner—you're the project manager, and your involvement is crucial to keeping the renovation on track.

Handling Delays and Unexpected Issues

Renovations rarely go exactly as planned, and delays or unexpected issues can occur. How you handle these situations will determine the overall success of your project. My advice is to stay calm and solution-focused. Rather than getting frustrated, work with your contractors to find the most efficient way to get back on track.

If an issue could significantly delay the project or increase costs, gather all the information before making a decision. Consider your options and adjust your plans to accommodate the changes if necessary.

Flexibility and patience are essential qualities in managing a successful renovation.

Final Walkthrough and Inspection

Before you sign off on the renovation, do a final walkthrough with your contractors. This is your opportunity to ensure that all work has been completed to your satisfaction and that any issues have been addressed. Be thorough in your inspection—check for quality and functionality and ensure that all renovations meet your original expectations.

If you find any discrepancies, don't hesitate to point them out. Contractors expect a punch list of final adjustments, so make sure everything is up to standard before you make the final payment. Once you're completely satisfied, you can celebrate the completion of your renovation and look forward to welcoming your new residents.

Renovating a property for co-living is a significant undertaking, but with proper planning, budgeting, and management, you can create a beautiful and functional space that meets the needs of your future residents. Remember, this is more than just a renovation—it's about transforming a property into a home where people can connect, share experiences, and live comfortably. By following these guidelines, you'll be well on your way to achieving a successful co-living renovation that exceeds your expectations.

CHAPTER 6

THE ART OF THE PERFECT LISTING: YOUR PATH TO FULL OCCUPANCY

"You never get a second chance to make a first impression."
— *Will Rogers*

The first impression your property makes on potential tenants isn't during a walk-through or a meet-and-greet—it's online. Your listing is the digital front door of your co-living space, and in today's market, it's often the deciding factor between a property that fills up in days and one that lingers with vacancies. A compelling listing doesn't just showcase your property; it tells a story, highlighting the lifestyle and community your tenants can expect. It's your opportunity to stand out in a crowded marketplace and attract high-quality tenants who will appreciate, respect, and enjoy the environment you've created.

But what makes a great listing? It's not just about slapping a few photos and a description together. The best listings combine professional visuals, engaging descriptions, and immersive tools to capture a tenant's imagination and make them eager to move in. Let's dive into how each element plays a crucial role in your success.

Staging: The Foundation of a Great Listing

Before a single photo is taken, the property must be staged. Imagine walking into a beautifully organized space where every piece of furniture feels intentional, and every room is inviting. Now imagine the opposite: a cluttered, mismatched space that feels cold and unwelcoming. Which one would you choose?

Staging sets the tone for the entire listing. It allows potential tenants to envision themselves living in the space and helps them connect emotionally to the property. Each bedroom should feel like a private retreat, with a cozy bed, functional workspace, and ample storage. In shared spaces, like the kitchen and dining area, you want to create an environment that encourages interaction while maintaining a sense of order. Comfortable seating, clean lines, and a few well-placed pops of color—think vibrant pillows or modern artwork—can make all the difference.

Outdoor spaces shouldn't be neglected either. A simple, inviting patio setup or a well-maintained garden can add a whole new dimension to the tenant experience, showing them that your property is more than just a place to sleep; it's a place to live.

Professional Photography: The Power of Visuals

Once your space is perfectly staged, it's time to capture it. In the world of online listings, photos are king. They're the first thing prospective tenants see, and they often determine whether someone clicks to learn more or keeps scrolling.

Professional photography ensures that your property is presented in the best possible light—literally. Good photographers understand how to use lighting to make spaces feel bright and welcoming. They know how to frame shots to highlight the flow of a room and capture the small details that make your property unique.

A series of high-resolution images showcasing each bedroom, shared space, and outdoor area will give potential tenants a comprehensive view of the property. Don't skimp on this step. Grainy, poorly lit photos can make even the most beautiful home look uninviting.

Virtual 3D Tours: Bringing the Property to Life

While photos are essential, they only tell part of the story. For tenants relocating from another city—or those who simply prefer a more interactive experience—virtual 3D tours are a game-changer.

Imagine being able to "walk" through a property from the comfort of your couch. Virtual tours provide an immersive experience, allowing potential tenants to explore every corner of your co-living space at their own pace. They can see how the bedrooms connect to the shared spaces, get a feel for the layout, and even check out the views from the windows.

This transparency builds trust and excitement. Tenants know exactly what they're getting, which can speed up decision-making and reduce the need for in-person showings. Plus, offering a 3D tour demonstrates that you're a modern, tech-savvy landlord who values convenience—a big plus for today's renters.

Crafting a Compelling Listing Description

Once the visuals are ready, it's time to put pen to paper—or fingers to keyboard. A great listing description does more than just list features; it paints a picture of what life in your co-living property is like.

Start by highlighting the unique features of the home:

"This fully renovated property offers seven private bedrooms, each designed with comfort and privacy in mind. Each room includes a cozy bed, a dedicated workspace, and ample storage, making it the perfect retreat after a busy day."

Then, focus on the shared spaces:

"The spacious kitchen is a chef's dream, equipped with modern appliances, plenty of prep space, and designated storage for each tenant. The open dining area is perfect for shared meals or late-night study sessions. Step outside to the cozy back patio, ideal for morning coffee or evening gatherings."

Next, sell the lifestyle:

"Located in a vibrant neighborhood, this home offers easy access to public transportation, grocery stores, and popular cafes. Whether you're commuting to work or exploring local hotspots, everything you need is just minutes away."

Finally, emphasize the benefits of co-living:

"Join a community of like-minded professionals who value both privacy and connection. With all utilities and services included in your rent, you can focus on what matters most while we handle the rest."

Neighborhood Amenities: Location, Location, Location

Don't underestimate the importance of selling the neighborhood. For many tenants, the surrounding area is just as important as the property itself. Highlight nearby conveniences like grocery stores, fitness centers, and public transit. Mention local attractions like parks, restaurants, or cultural hotspots.

When potential tenants see that your property offers not only a great living space but also access to a thriving, convenient neighborhood, it becomes even more appealing.

Setting Rental Rates, Tenant Screening, and Lease Agreements

Setting the right rental rates and creating a solid tenant screening process are crucial to operating a successful co-living property. You want to strike a balance between affordability for tenants and profitability for your business.

Determining Competitive Rental Rates

Setting rental rates is a balancing act. You need to consider the market rates in your area, the amenities you offer, and your overall expenses. I suggest conducting a market analysis to understand what similar properties in your area are charging. This will give you a baseline to work with when determining your rates.

Remember that co-living often appeals to people looking for a more affordable housing option, so it's important to remain competitive.

Offering a range of pricing options for different room types or levels of privacy can attract a wider variety of tenants. For example, you might offer lower rates for shared rooms and higher rates for private en-suite rooms.

Factoring in Utilities and Additional Costs

When setting your rental rates, don't forget to factor in the cost of utilities, maintenance, and any additional services you plan to offer. Many co-living properties include utilities like electricity, water, and Wi-Fi in the rent, which can be a big selling point for tenants. If you include these costs, ensure your rates reflect the added value.

You can also consider charging extra for optional services like cleaning, laundry, or premium Wi-Fi. This will increase your revenue and give tenants the flexibility to choose the services that best meet their needs.

Tenant Screening Process

The tenant screening process is one of the most critical steps in ensuring the success of your co-living property. It's not just about finding someone who can reliably pay rent; it's about selecting individuals who will contribute positively to the shared living environment. A harmonious household starts with thoughtful tenant selection, and that begins with a thorough and deliberate screening process.

When evaluating prospective tenants, it's important to dig deeper than just their financial qualifications. A background check can reveal any red flags that might affect the safety or comfort of other residents, while a credit check offers insight into their financial responsibility and ability to meet rent obligations. But beyond these formalities, speaking with previous landlords or employers can provide valuable context about their rental history and reliability.

In addition to verifying a tenant's ability to pay rent, it's equally vital to ensure they understand and are prepared for the realities of co-living. Many people are unfamiliar with the unique dynamics of shared housing, so part of the screening process should include a clear explanation of what co-living entails. This is your opportunity to set expectations and make sure applicants are comfortable with the concept of sharing spaces, following communal rules, and respecting the privacy and boundaries of others.

House rules play a crucial role in maintaining a peaceful and functional co-living environment, and these should be introduced early in the screening process. Whether it's quiet hours, cleaning schedules, or guidelines for hosting guests, these rules provide the structure that allows a diverse group of people to live together harmoniously. Prospective tenants should be given a copy of the house rules and asked to review them carefully. Then, as part of the application process, they should confirm their understanding and agreement to abide by them. This simple step helps filter out individuals who may not be suited for co-living, saving you potential headaches down the road.

Beyond the formalities, take time to have a conversation with each applicant. This is where you can gauge their personality and attitude toward communal living. Ask about their past experiences in shared spaces, how they handle conflicts, and what they're looking for in a living arrangement. Their answers will give you a sense of whether they're likely to fit in with the existing community. Co-living thrives on respect, cooperation, and a shared commitment to maintaining a positive environment, so finding tenants who align with these values is essential.

In the end, tenant screening is about more than just filling rooms; it's about building a community. By thoroughly vetting applicants and setting clear expectations from the start, you create a living environment where residents feel safe, respected, and at home. This proactive approach not only enhances tenant satisfaction but also ensures the long-term success and stability of your co-living property.

Creating a Clear Lease Agreement

A well-drafted lease agreement is one of the most important tools in your arsenal as a co-living property operator. It's not just a legal document—it's the framework for your relationship with your tenants.

A clear and comprehensive lease agreement helps ensure that everyone is on the same page from day one, minimizing misunderstandings and setting the stage for a harmonious living arrangement.

When crafting your lease, think of it as a roadmap that guides tenants through their responsibilities and rights while living in your property. Start with the basics: the rental amount, payment due dates, and the duration of the lease. These fundamental terms lay the groundwork, but they're only the beginning. A truly effective lease goes beyond the surface to address the finer details that often cause disputes.

Consider the security deposit, for example. Tenants need to know not only the amount but also the conditions under which it will be returned—or withheld. Spell out what constitutes acceptable wear and tear versus damage, and make it clear how and when the deposit will be refunded. This transparency helps prevent misunderstandings when the lease ends and gives tenants clear guidelines for maintaining the space.

Next, think about the day-to-day rules that keep a co-living environment running smoothly. Policies around guest visits, quiet hours, and the use of shared spaces like kitchens and laundry rooms should be detailed in the lease. Tenants should know exactly what's expected of them and what the consequences are for failing to adhere to these rules. For example, if your property has strict quiet hours, specify the times and the types of activities that are restricted. If you have a limit on how long guests can stay, include that as well. These specifics ensure that everyone understands the house rules from the start.

Equally important are clauses addressing what happens in case of lease violations or early termination. Life is unpredictable, and sometimes tenants may need to break their lease due to unforeseen circumstances. Your agreement should outline the steps they need to take, whether it's providing a certain amount of notice or paying a termination fee. Similarly, if a tenant violates house rules—be it consistent noise complaints, failure to pay rent, or disruptive behavior—you need to have a clear, enforceable process for addressing the situation.

A strong lease also covers the unique aspects of co-living. For instance, tenants should be aware that they're not just renting a room; they're sharing common areas with others. This includes clear language about responsibilities for keeping shared spaces clean and functional. If your property provides utilities, Wi-Fi, or housekeeping as part of the rental package, specify the details, such as whether there are usage limits or additional charges for overages.

It's also a good idea to include a section about conflict resolution. Co-living spaces are, by nature, communal, and occasional disputes are inevitable. Having a predefined process for resolving disagreements— whether it's through mediation, a tenant meeting, or involving a property manager—can prevent small issues from escalating into major conflicts.

The clearer and more detailed your lease agreement, the easier it will be to manage expectations and handle any issues that arise. Tenants appreciate knowing exactly where they stand, and you'll benefit from having a solid, enforceable document to reference if disputes occur. Ultimately, a well-crafted lease protects both parties, ensuring a smoother, more predictable rental experience for everyone involved.

Leveraging Platform Tools and Monitoring Performance with PadSplit

One of the standout advantages of listing your co-living property on a platform like PadSplit is the robust suite of tools it offers to streamline the rental process. From tenant acquisition to performance tracking, PadSplit simplifies the operational side of property management, allowing you to focus on maintaining a high-quality living environment. These tools don't just save time; they provide invaluable insights that can help you maximize occupancy and attract the right tenants quickly.

Streamlined Tenant Vetting and Leasing

PadSplit takes much of the heavy lifting out of tenant screening and leasing, handling processes that might otherwise consume a significant portion of your time. The platform conducts thorough background checks, including criminal and credit history, to ensure that applicants meet stringent criteria. This vetting process helps maintain a safe and reliable tenant pool, giving you peace of mind about the residents moving into your property.

Additionally, PadSplit manages the entire leasing process. Once a tenant is approved, the platform provides a standardized lease agreement tailored to the co-living model. This agreement is clear, comprehensive, and designed to set expectations from the outset. By taking care of these critical steps, PadSplit allows you to bypass the administrative complexities while ensuring that all legal and operational bases are covered.

Performance Tracking and Data Insights

PadSplit offers detailed analytics that provide a real-time view of how your property is performing. These insights help you make informed decisions to optimize your listing and ensure maximum occupancy.

Key Metrics Include:

- **Listing Views and Engagement**: See how many people are viewing your listing and gauge the level of interest. If engagement is low, it might be time to update your photos or tweak your description.

- **Inquiries and Applications**: Track how many viewers are converting into inquiries and applications. High views but low applications could indicate that your pricing or amenities need adjusting.

- **Occupancy Rates**: Monitor your occupancy over time to identify trends and anticipate future vacancies.

By regularly reviewing these metrics, you can adjust your approach as needed to keep your property competitive. For instance, if your listing isn't performing as expected, PadSplit's tools might suggest actionable improvements, such as updating photos, refining your description, or even adjusting pricing based on market trends.

Dynamic Pricing Recommendations

Another powerful feature is PadSplit's dynamic pricing tool, which helps you stay competitive without undercutting your profitability. The platform provides data-driven pricing recommendations based on local market conditions, seasonal trends, and demand. This ensures your property is always priced to attract tenants while maximizing revenue.

Listing Optimization Suggestions

Based on performance data, PadSplit provides actionable suggestions for improving your listing. These might include:

- **Photo Enhancements**: Recommendations to update or add specific types of photos, such as clearer bedroom shots or showcasing newly updated amenities.

- **Description Tweaks**: Suggestions for emphasizing features that attract tenants, like highlighting proximity to public transit, including details about recently upgraded appliances, or spotlighting shared amenities like high-speed internet or a furnished patio.

- **Call-to-Action Improvements**: Guidance on making your listing's calls-to-action more compelling, encouraging potential tenants to inquire or apply immediately.

Incentive Management

To boost interest, PadSplit allows you to offer incentives like a discounted first month's rent or waiving certain fees for tenants who apply within a specific timeframe. These promotions can be a powerful tool to drive urgency and attract tenants during slower periods.

Best Practices for Incentives:

- **Limited-Time Offers**: Clearly communicate deadlines to create a sense of urgency.

- **Seasonal Discounts**: Use these strategically during off-peak seasons to maintain steady occupancy.

- **Referral Bonuses**: Encourage current tenants to refer friends or colleagues by offering them rewards, further strengthening your community while filling vacancies.

Continuous Support and Insights

PadSplit doesn't just provide tools—it also offers ongoing support through dedicated account managers and educational resources. These resources can help you navigate challenges, optimize your listings, and stay informed about co-living best practices.

Data-Driven Success

Leveraging PadSplit's platform tools ensures that you're not just listing a property—you're strategically marketing it to attract the right tenants quickly and efficiently. By monitoring performance, optimizing your listings, and using the platform's automated and data-driven features, you can achieve full occupancy in record time while maintaining a high standard of tenant satisfaction. This proactive, tech-savvy approach is key to staying competitive in the co-living market.

The Key to Full Occupancy

In the world of co-living, your listing isn't just an advertisement—it's an invitation. It sets the tone for the living experience you offer and serves as the first point of contact between your property and prospective tenants. A well-crafted listing does more than inform; it captivates, inspires, and builds trust. By investing in key elements like staging, professional photography, virtual tours, and compelling descriptions, you're not merely showcasing a space—you're presenting a lifestyle.

The competitive rental market demands excellence. Every detail, from the way light filters through a staged room to the warmth conveyed in your listing description, plays a role in setting your property apart. High-quality tenants are not just looking for a place to sleep; they're seeking a home that offers comfort, security, community, and convenience. Your listing must reflect these values, showing them that you've thought through every aspect of their living experience.

When potential tenants see a property that's well-maintained, thoughtfully designed, and marketed with care, it signals more than just aesthetic appeal—it shows them you're a conscientious landlord who prioritizes their well-being. This level of professionalism and attention to detail reassures tenants that their needs will be met and their concerns addressed, making them eager to join your community.

Ultimately, a great listing doesn't just fill rooms; it attracts the right residents—those who will respect the space, appreciate the community, and stay long-term. By leveraging the power of a standout listing, you can achieve full occupancy faster, reduce turnover, and create a thriving, harmonious co-living environment that benefits both your tenants and your bottom line.

CHAPTER 7

OPERATING A PROFITABLE CO-LIVING PROPERTY

"The secret of success is to do the common thing uncommonly well."
— *John D. Rockefeller*

Operating a co-living space is more than just managing a property—it's akin to running a small business where your product is a lifestyle that balances community living with individual comfort. Whether you operate independently or under an existing co-living platform, success hinges on providing more than just a place to stay. You're creating a living experience that prioritizes comfort, safety, security, and a strong sense of community. Each of these elements requires thoughtful planning and consistent effort to meet the unique needs of your residents.

Managing a co-living property, whether you're just starting with your first investment property or managing multiple properties with the help of a property manager, requires more than a passive approach. Success lies in creating a structured, repeatable routine that keeps the property running smoothly and residents happy. Routine is the backbone of effective property management—it ensures nothing falls through the cracks and that every aspect of the property is maintained proactively.

For first-time co-living operators, I strongly recommend self-managing your property to gain hands-on experience. This gives you a deeper understanding of the daily operations, the needs of your tenants, and the challenges involved. Once you've scaled and brought on a property manager, the systems and routines you establish early on will serve as a blueprint for consistent and efficient operations across your portfolio.

Creating a Routine for Property Management

Effective management of a co-living space hinges on creating a structured routine that ensures the property runs smoothly. Whether you're managing the property yourself or delegating to a property manager, having a well-defined plan helps maintain consistency and prevents small issues from becoming larger, costly problems.

A solid routine enables you to stay proactive. By conducting regular inspections of common areas—such as kitchens, bathrooms, and outdoor spaces—you can spot potential maintenance needs early, often before tenants even notice. This not only keeps the property in top condition but also minimizes disruptions for your tenants, fostering a more positive living experience. Addressing issues promptly and efficiently signals to residents that their comfort and well-being are priorities, which ultimately enhances tenant satisfaction and retention.

The Power of Checklists

Checklists are your best friend in property management. They keep you organized, ensure tasks are completed consistently, and provide a clear record of what's been done. Here's how they can be applied:

- **Daily Tasks**: Checking that common areas are clean, ensuring all appliances are functioning, and addressing any immediate tenant requests.
- **Weekly Tasks**: Inspecting high-traffic areas like kitchens and bathrooms for wear and tear, checking for signs of pests, and ensuring outdoor areas are tidy.
- **Monthly Tasks**: Testing smoke detectors, checking plumbing for leaks, reviewing tenant feedback, and updating maintenance logs.
- **Seasonal Tasks**: Preparing HVAC systems for changes in weather, inspecting roofs and gutters, and scheduling deep cleanings or larger repairs.

For those self-managing their first property, these checklists will help you stay on top of everything without feeling overwhelmed. For those with property managers, sharing these checklists ensures that your standards are upheld, and you can easily monitor their work.

Proactive Maintenance: Staying Ahead of Problems

A significant part of operating a successful co-living property is being proactive rather than reactive. Waiting for tenants to report problems often means small issues have already escalated. Instead, regular checks and routine maintenance allow you to catch things early, reducing repair costs and minimizing disruptions for tenants.

Key Areas to Monitor Regularly:

- **Kitchens and Bathrooms**: These high-use areas require frequent inspections. Check for leaks, clogs, or signs of mold, and ensure all appliances and fixtures are in working order.
- **Outdoor Spaces**: Ensure porches, patios, and yards are well-maintained. Clear any debris, check for loose railings or damaged steps, and ensure lighting is functional.

- **HVAC Systems**: Regularly replace filters and schedule seasonal inspections to ensure heating and cooling systems are running efficiently.

Proactive maintenance keeps the property in top condition and shows tenants that you care about their living environment, which enhances tenant satisfaction and retention.

Tenant Interaction: Clear Communication and Prompt Responses

Tenants are the lifeblood of your co-living property, and maintaining open lines of communication is critical to ensuring they feel heard and valued.

Establishing Communication Channels:

- **Dedicated Messaging System**: Use platforms that centralize tenant communications, such as property management software or even group chats, to streamline requests and updates.
- **Office Hours**: Even if you're self-managing, set clear hours when tenants can expect a response. This establishes boundaries while ensuring their concerns are addressed promptly.

- **Regular Check-Ins**: Periodic surveys or informal check-ins show tenants that you're proactive about their experience and willing to make improvements based on their feedback.

Delegation and Oversight: Scaling with Property Managers

As your portfolio grows, you may transition from self-managing to working with a property manager. While this alleviates some of the hands-on responsibilities, it doesn't mean you should step back entirely. The systems and routines you've established should guide their work, ensuring consistency across all properties.

Oversight Best Practices:

- **Weekly Reports**: Require your property manager to provide regular updates, including completed tasks, tenant feedback, and any ongoing issues.
- **Performance Reviews**: Periodically review their performance against your established routines and checklists to ensure your standards are being met.
- **Ongoing Training**: Provide opportunities for your property manager to learn and improve, whether through formal training or by sharing your own insights and experience.

The Benefits of a Structured Routine

A well-structured routine has far-reaching benefits:

- **Minimized Downtime**: Proactive maintenance reduces the likelihood of major repairs, ensuring the property remains operational and appealing to tenants.

- **Improved Tenant Satisfaction**: Tenants appreciate a well-maintained property and prompt responses to their concerns, leading to longer stays and fewer vacancies.

- **Streamlined Operations**: With checklists and routines in place, even complex tasks become manageable, whether you're self-managing or working with a property manager.

- **Enhanced Property Value**: Regular upkeep and maintenance protect your investment, keeping the property in excellent condition for years to come.

Operating a successful co-living property requires a mix of organization, attention to detail, and proactive management. Whether you're self-managing your first property or overseeing a growing portfolio with the help of a property manager, the routines and systems you establish will set you up for long-term success. By staying organized, anticipating issues, and maintaining clear communication with tenants, you'll create a thriving co-living environment that attracts and retains high-quality residents.

Handling Tenant Disputes and Maintaining a Community Feel

Even in the best-managed co-living spaces, tenant disputes are bound to happen. When people with different lifestyles, habits, and expectations share a home, occasional friction is inevitable. However, how you address these conflicts can make or break the community atmosphere of your property. A proactive, empathetic approach not only resolves disputes effectively but also strengthens the sense of camaraderie among tenants.

Addressing Conflicts Early: Nipping Problems in the Bud

One of the most important principles in conflict resolution is to act quickly. In a co-living environment, small misunderstandings—whether over cleaning duties, noise levels, or guest policies—can escalate into larger issues if left unchecked. Early intervention is key to preventing resentment and maintaining harmony within the household.

To make this process seamless, establish a protocol that encourages tenants to report conflicts as soon as they arise. Let them know that their concerns will be taken seriously and addressed promptly. When disputes come to your attention, schedule a time to talk with the involved parties individually, ensuring they feel heard without fear of judgment. Then, bring them together for a mediated discussion. Often, what appears to be a serious conflict can be resolved through open communication, with both sides gaining a better understanding of each other's perspectives.

For example, a tenant might be frustrated about a roommate frequently hosting guests late at night, while the host tenant might not have realized how disruptive it was. By facilitating a respectful conversation, you can help them agree on boundaries that work for both parties—like limiting guest visits to certain hours or giving advance notice.

Setting Clear House Rules: The Foundation of Peaceful Co-Living

Many disputes can be avoided altogether by establishing clear, well-communicated house rules. These guidelines set expectations for communal living and help tenants navigate shared responsibilities. Rules should cover common areas of conflict, such as:

- **Quiet Hours**: Specify times when noise should be kept to a minimum.
- **Guest Policies**: Define how often tenants can have guests and for how long.
- **Cleaning Responsibilities**: Detail how shared spaces like kitchens and bathrooms should be maintained and by whom.

- **Shared Space Etiquette**: Clarify expectations for the use of communal areas, such as the living room or laundry facilities.

Include these rules in the lease agreement and go over them during tenant orientation. For added visibility, post them in shared spaces like the kitchen or hallway. Consistently enforcing these rules is crucial; if tenants see that violations are overlooked, they may lose respect for the guidelines, leading to more frequent conflicts.

By having a clear framework, you provide tenants with a sense of structure. When disagreements arise, you can refer back to the rules, reinforcing that they are there to support fairness and harmony in the household.

Encouraging Open Communication: Building Trust and Community

Fostering open communication among tenants is another critical element in maintaining a peaceful co-living environment. When people feel they can express their concerns without fear of retaliation, they are more likely to address minor annoyances before they become major grievances.

Create multiple channels for tenants to share their thoughts. Regular tenant meetings are an excellent opportunity for residents to discuss issues collectively, propose improvements, or share positive feedback.

If in-person meetings aren't feasible, consider using a digital platform like a group chat or a dedicated message board. For those who prefer anonymity, a suggestion box can provide a safe space to voice concerns.

Open communication doesn't just resolve conflicts—it strengthens the community. When tenants feel heard and respected, they're more likely to collaborate on solutions and support each other in maintaining a positive living environment. This sense of mutual respect is what transforms a group of individuals sharing a house into a cohesive, supportive community.

Mediation and Problem-Solving: A Neutral Approach to Resolution

In some cases, disputes may require more formal mediation. As the property owner or manager, you can step in as a neutral party to facilitate a structured discussion. Your role is not to take sides but to guide the conversation in a way that helps tenants articulate their concerns, understand each other's viewpoints, and work toward a fair compromise.

For instance, if two tenants consistently clash over cleaning duties, you could propose a rotating schedule that accommodates both parties' preferences. If the issue is more personal—like a perceived lack of respect or privacy—help them establish clear boundaries and communication strategies to avoid future misunderstandings.

Mediation not only resolves the immediate conflict but also equips tenants with the tools to handle similar issues independently in the future. It reinforces the idea that conflicts are a natural part of communal living and that they can be resolved constructively.

The Benefits of Proactive Conflict Management

Addressing disputes effectively does more than restore peace; it enhances the overall living experience. Tenants who feel their concerns are taken seriously and resolved fairly are more likely to remain in the property long-term. They'll also be more inclined to contribute positively to the community, whether by maintaining shared spaces, supporting new tenants, or simply fostering a friendly atmosphere.

By taking a proactive approach to conflict resolution—through early intervention, clear house rules, open communication, and structured mediation—you create a living environment where tenants feel valued, respected, and connected. This not only benefits the current residents but also strengthens your property's reputation, making it more attractive to future tenants. In the end, a harmonious co-living space is a testament to thoughtful management and a commitment to fostering community.

Building a Thriving Co-Living Community

Operating a successful and profitable co-living property requires more than just filling rooms—it demands strong management, careful tenant selection, and a commitment to creating a positive living environment. By focusing on these core principles, you'll not only meet your financial goals but also cultivate a space where tenants feel comfortable, respected, and connected.

Whether you're self-managing your first property or overseeing a portfolio with the help of a property manager, the systems and routines you establish will lay the foundation for long-term success. Thoughtful tenant screening ensures a harmonious community, while proactive management keeps operations running smoothly. At the heart of it all is your dedication to providing an exceptional co-living experience—one that tenants value and are happy to call home.

CHAPTER 8

SCALING YOUR CO-LIVING PORTFOLIO

"We keep moving forward, opening new doors, and doing new things, because we're curious and curiosity keeps leading us down new paths."

– Walt Disney

Once you've successfully launched your first co-living property, you've likely gained invaluable experience in managing operations, creating a harmonious tenant community, and maintaining a profitable venture. With a solid foundation in place, the natural next step is to think bigger: scaling your co-living portfolio. Expanding your operations is an exciting milestone, offering the potential for increased revenue, greater impact, and the opportunity to establish yourself as a leader in the co-living space. However, growth also comes with its own set of challenges and complexities.

Scaling isn't just about acquiring more properties; it's about replicating your success while refining your processes to handle a larger operation. This chapter will guide you through the critical elements of expansion, from building a reliable team to exploring diverse property types and markets. You'll learn how to transition from being hands-on in every aspect of your first property to effectively delegating tasks and managing a broader portfolio strategically.

We'll also discuss the benefits of diversifying your investments. Whether it's expanding into different neighborhoods, experimenting with various housing types, or tailoring properties to different tenant demographics, diversification helps mitigate risks while tapping into new revenue streams. With the right approach, scaling can not only amplify your profits but also create a lasting impact on the communities you serve.

In the following pages, we'll delve into the strategies and best practices for expanding your co-living business, equipping you with the tools to grow sustainably and confidently. The journey to scaling your portfolio is an exciting challenge, and with careful planning and execution, you'll be well-positioned to maximize your success in the co-living market.

Assessing Your Current Success

Before diving headfirst into expansion, it's crucial to take a step back and thoroughly evaluate the performance of your existing property. Think of this as laying the foundation for your future growth. Without a clear understanding of what's working and what needs improvement, you risk replicating mistakes rather than success.

Start by analyzing key performance metrics such as:

- **Occupancy Rates**: Are your units consistently full? High occupancy indicates strong demand and effective marketing.

- **Tenant Turnover**: How often do tenants leave? Low turnover is a good sign of tenant satisfaction and a well-managed property.

- **Profitability**: Is your property generating the expected returns? Review your income and expenses to ensure you're meeting your financial goals.

- **Tenant Satisfaction**: What are your tenants saying? Feedback from tenant surveys or informal check-ins can provide valuable insights into their experience.

For example, if your tenants consistently praise the property's sense of community but express concerns about maintenance delays, you know to prioritize operational efficiency in your next venture. Conversely, if occupancy fluctuates, you might need to refine your marketing strategy before expanding. The performance of your first property sets the benchmark for your future investments—use this data to guide your decisions.

Choosing the Right Location for Expansion

Location remains a critical factor in the success of any co-living property. Just as you carefully selected the location for your first property, you'll need to be equally diligent when choosing your next. Expanding into the right neighborhood can significantly boost your chances of success and profitability.

Replicating Your Success Formula

Scaling a co-living portfolio isn't just about acquiring more properties; it's about replicating the elements that made your first property successful while adapting to new challenges. To ensure consistency across your portfolio, it's essential to develop standardized operating procedures (SOPs) that outline every aspect of property management.

What Should Your SOPs Cover?

- **Tenant Onboarding**: Standardize the process of welcoming new tenants, from lease agreements to introducing house rules and community guidelines.
- **Community Building**: Outline how to foster a sense of community, such as organizing regular events or creating shared spaces that encourage interaction.
- **Maintenance Schedules**: Implement a system for routine checks and timely repairs to keep the property in top condition.

- **Conflict Resolution**: Establish a clear process for handling tenant disputes to maintain harmony in the household.

Take a moment to reflect on the unique factors that contributed to your first property's success. Was it the thoughtful design of shared spaces? The variety of amenities? Or perhaps the emphasis on building a strong tenant community? Whatever those key elements were, make them a cornerstone of your expansion strategy. For instance, if tenants loved the co-working space in your first property, consider including similar features in your next venture.

Balancing Standardization and Flexibility

While consistency is crucial, scaling also requires a degree of flexibility. Each property will have its unique characteristics based on its location, tenant demographic, and layout. While your SOPs provide a framework, be prepared to adapt them to meet the specific needs of each property.

For example, a property in a bustling urban area might benefit from amenities like secure bike storage or proximity to public transportation, while a suburban property could focus more on outdoor spaces and parking facilities. Tailoring your approach while maintaining your brand's core values ensures that each property remains competitive and relevant to its market.

◆◆◆

Maria's Journey to Scaling Her Co-Living Portfolio

Maria had successfully launched her first co-living property in a bustling university district. With consistently high occupancy rates and positive feedback from her tenants, she knew she had tapped into a thriving market. Her property offered more than just affordable housing; it provided a sense of community, complete with thoughtfully designed common spaces and regular social events. Encouraged by her initial success, Maria decided it was time to scale her portfolio.

Before moving forward, Maria conducted a thorough review of her first property's performance. She looked at key metrics: occupancy rates were consistently above 95%, indicating strong demand; tenant turnover was low, with most tenants renewing their leases or staying for the full term. However, tenant surveys revealed some recurring feedback: while residents loved the community vibe and amenities, a few had raised concerns about delayed maintenance requests. Recognizing this as an area for improvement, Maria prioritized streamlining her maintenance processes for her next properties.

Choosing the Right Location

Maria knew that location would be critical to her expansion. She began by researching several neighborhoods that aligned with her target demographics. One area stood out: a tech hub experiencing rapid growth, attracting young professionals looking for flexible, affordable housing. The local real estate market showed promising trends—rising rental rates and increasing demand for shared housing.

Maria also identified another promising neighborhood near a healthcare district with several major hospitals. This area attracted traveling nurses and medical residents, a demographic that aligned perfectly with the co-living model due to their need for short-term, community-oriented housing.

After careful consideration, Maria decided to invest in properties in both neighborhoods, confident that diversifying her portfolio across different tenant demographics would mitigate risk and maximize profitability.

Replicating and Refining Her Success Formula

Maria understood that the key to scaling was maintaining the elements that had made her first property successful while tailoring each new property to its unique market. She developed a set of standardized operating procedures (SOPs) to ensure consistency across all locations. These SOPs covered everything from tenant onboarding to community-building strategies and maintenance schedules.

At her tech hub property, Maria incorporated private co-working spaces and high-speed internet to cater to remote workers. She also introduced regular networking events to foster connections among tenants. For the healthcare district property, Maria emphasized flexible lease terms and created quiet, comfortable communal spaces ideal for tenants with demanding work schedules.

Maria also leveraged feedback from her first property to improve operational efficiency. She partnered with a local maintenance company to provide faster response times for repair requests and implemented a digital system that allowed tenants to submit and track maintenance issues in real-time.

Balancing Standardization with Flexibility

Maria's ability to adapt while maintaining her core values was crucial to her success. While her SOPs ensured a consistent tenant experience across all properties, she tailored her approach to each location's specific needs.

For instance, the tech hub property offered amenities like secure bike storage and easy access to public transportation, catering to eco-conscious professionals. Meanwhile, her suburban property focused on offering larger private rooms and ample parking, appealing to tenants who preferred a quieter environment with more personal space.

This balance of standardization and flexibility allowed Maria to scale her business without compromising on quality or tenant satisfaction.

Results of Scaling Smartly

Within two years, Maria had expanded her portfolio to include four co-living properties, each thriving in its unique way. Her tech hub property consistently attracted remote workers and young professionals, maintaining a 98% occupancy rate. Her healthcare district property became a sought-after option for traveling nurses, with flexible leases that perfectly matched their needs.

By leveraging her initial success and refining her model with each new property, Maria was able to replicate her winning formula while adapting to different markets. Her focus on community, efficient operations, and tailored amenities ensured that each property offered an exceptional living experience. As a result, Maria not only grew her business but also built a reputation as a leader in the co-living industry, known for creating vibrant, well-managed communities where tenants felt at home.

◆ ◆ ◆

Financial Planning for Expansion

Scaling begins with a robust financial plan. Whether you're acquiring your second property or your tenth, a detailed budget is essential. Your plan should encompass every aspect of the expansion, from acquisition costs and renovation expenses to furnishing, marketing, and operational setup. This level of detail ensures you have a clear picture of your financial needs and helps you project your return on investment (ROI) for each property.

Expansion often requires significant capital. To avoid overstretching your resources, explore different financing options such as traditional bank loans, private investors, or crowdfunding campaigns. Each option has its advantages and considerations, and the right choice depends on your financial position and growth goals. Scaling your portfolio is a long-term endeavor, so it's important to pace yourself to maintain financial stability.

Marketing Your New Co-Living Spaces

Once your new co-living property is ready, attracting tenants becomes the next priority. A robust marketing strategy ensures high occupancy rates from the start. Digital marketing channels, such as social media, property listing websites, and your own website, are powerful tools for creating buzz around your new location.

Highlight the unique features of your property. Use high-quality photos, virtual tours, and testimonials from current tenants to showcase the lifestyle your co-living property offers.

Word-of-mouth marketing can also be highly effective. Encourage your existing tenants to refer friends by offering referral incentives. Satisfied tenants can be your most effective ambassadors, helping you fill vacancies quickly while reinforcing the sense of community within your properties.

Building a Team to Support Your Growth

As your portfolio grows, managing everything independently becomes increasingly challenging. Building a capable team is essential to streamline operations, enhance tenant experiences, and scale efficiently.

Start by defining the roles you need to fill. Property management, tenant relations, marketing, maintenance, and finance are all critical areas that require dedicated attention. Hiring a property manager allows you to delegate day-to-day operations, while a marketing specialist can focus on attracting tenants. A financial analyst helps monitor the performance of your properties, and a maintenance supervisor ensures all locations remain in top condition.

Hiring the right people is about more than technical skills—it's about finding individuals who align with your vision and values. In the co-living industry, it's crucial to have a team that understands the importance of community and works to create a positive living environment.

Promoting a positive team culture is equally important. Open communication and professional growth opportunities help keep your team engaged and aligned with your mission. A motivated team will not only excel in their roles but also contribute to building a strong community within your co-living spaces.

Diversifying Your Investments

Diversification is a powerful strategy for mitigating risk and maximizing returns. Expanding into different housing types or markets allows you to attract a broader range of tenants and build a more resilient portfolio.

Consider branching into models like micro-apartments, student housing, or shared office spaces. These options often cater to similar demographics—young professionals, digital nomads, or students—but offer different revenue streams.

Before diversifying, analyze market trends to identify gaps in housing demand. Tailor your properties to meet these needs. For instance, if remote work is on the rise, consider creating co-living spaces with private workstations and reliable internet.

Leveraging Partnerships and Adapting to Market Trends

Scaling often involves significant capital, and partnerships can be a valuable resource. Joint ventures with other investors or developers allow you to share costs, risks, and expertise. Collaborating with like-minded partners can open doors to new opportunities and accelerate your growth.

Staying attuned to market trends is equally important. As tenant preferences shift, adapt your properties accordingly. Whether incorporating green technologies or adding luxury amenities, staying flexible ensures your properties remain competitive and desirable.

Building a Sustainable Growth Strategy

Ultimately, scaling your co-living portfolio is about sustainable growth. Rapid expansion without a solid foundation can lead to operational inefficiencies and financial strain. Focus on quality over quantity, continuously refine your processes, and prioritize tenant satisfaction.

With careful planning, a dedicated team, and a willingness to adapt, you can grow your co-living business into a thriving, impactful enterprise that offers exceptional living experiences and long-term profitability.

CHAPTER 9

BUILDING A STANDOUT BRAND FOR YOUR CO-LIVING BUSINESS

"Your brand is what other people say about you when you're not in the room."
— Jeff Bezos

Effective marketing and branding are about more than just filling vacancies—they're about creating a lasting impression that resonates with potential tenants and sets your co-living properties apart in a competitive market. A recognizable brand not only attracts the right tenants but also fosters a sense of community and loyalty that keeps your properties thriving. This chapter will guide you through the essential steps of developing a compelling brand and implementing marketing strategies that drive success.

Building a Brand for Your Co-Living Property

Branding is the foundation of your co-living business. It's not just about a catchy name or an eye-catching logo; it's about the experience you offer and the values you stand for. A strong brand communicates what makes your properties unique and why tenants should choose your spaces over others.

Defining Your Unique Identity

The first step in building a recognizable brand is identifying your target audience and what sets your co-living property apart. Are you catering to young professionals seeking flexible living arrangements near urban centers? Or are you targeting students who need affordable, community-oriented housing close to campus? Each demographic has distinct needs and preferences, and your brand should reflect those.

Consider the key attributes you want your brand to embody. For instance:

- **Community-Focused**: Highlight shared spaces that foster connections.
- **Quality and Comfort**: Showcase premium amenities, such as high-end finishes, private bathrooms, or shared working spaces with coffee/tea stations.
- **Affordability**: Promote cost-effective living with all-inclusive rent and shared resources.

Your branding should consistently convey these values across all touchpoints, from your website and social media to in-person interactions with tenants.

Crafting a Visual Identity

A consistent visual identity helps build recognition and trust. Develop a logo, color palette, and design elements that reflect your brand's personality. Use these elements across all marketing materials, including your website, social media profiles, brochures, and property signage.

High-quality images are essential for showcasing your co-living spaces. Photos of well-designed rooms, vibrant communal areas, and happy tenants create a strong emotional connection with potential renters. Consider investing in professional photography and even virtual tours to provide an immersive experience.

Developing Your Unique Value Proposition (UVP)

Your UVP should succinctly explain why tenants should choose your co-living property. Whether it's "affordable luxury with a vibrant community" or "sustainable living for modern professionals," your UVP should be a central theme in your marketing efforts. Display it prominently on your website, social media, and promotional materials to reinforce your brand's core message.

Storytelling: Bringing Your Brand to Life

People connect with stories, and your co-living brand has a unique story to tell. Share the journey of your properties—how they came to be, the community you've built, and the positive impact you've had on tenants' lives.

Tenant Testimonials and Experiences

Highlight the voices of your tenants. Personal stories and testimonials provide social proof and make your brand relatable. Feature these on your website, in videos, or as part of a social media series. Potential tenants are more likely to trust the experiences of current residents.

Content Creation

Create engaging content that aligns with your brand's mission. Blog posts, social media updates, and newsletters can focus on topics such as co-living benefits, tips for harmonious shared living, or profiles of community events. This positions you as an authority in the co-living space and keeps your audience engaged.

Macarena García

◆ ◆ ◆

Property Daughters: The Power of Soft Femininity in Co-Living

Property Daughters, founded by Macarena García, has carved a unique space in the co-living market by embracing a brand ethos of soft femininity. Rooted in warmth, elegance, and inclusivity, Property Daughters offers more than just housing; it creates a nurturing environment where tenants feel at home and connected. This distinctive approach has not only attracted a loyal tenant base but also set the brand apart in an industry often driven by functional, utilitarian design.

A Vision of Elegance and Comfort

From its inception, Property Daughters aimed to redefine co-living by integrating the principles of soft femininity into every aspect of the tenant experience. The brand's name itself evokes a sense of care, familial bonds, and empowerment. Macarena envisioned spaces that blended modern amenities with delicate design elements—creating homes that are both functional and inviting.

The properties under Property Daughters feature soft color palettes of blush tones, creams, and light grays, paired with elegant furnishings and thoughtful decor. Silk flowers in common areas, tasteful art, and natural light play a crucial role in crafting a serene atmosphere. These details reflect the brand's dedication to creating spaces that offer more than just utility—they offer solace and inspiration.

Building a Brand That Resonates

Property Daughters' branding extends beyond aesthetics. Its tagline, "Living beautifully, together," emphasizes its mission to foster community and shared experiences while maintaining personal comfort and style. The visual identity is soft yet strong, with delicate fonts and pastel hues reinforcing the brand's core message of elegance and togetherness.

The marketing strategy focuses on storytelling and visual narratives that capture the essence of life in a Property Daughters home. Social media posts showcase serene, shared spaces, highlight tenant connections, and feature testimonials that speak to the sense of belonging the brand cultivates.

A Rising Leader in Co-Living

Property Daughters' approach has proven highly effective. Occupancy rates remain consistently high, and tenant feedback highlights the unique blend of beauty, comfort, and community. The brand has quickly established itself as a leader in the Atlanta co-living market, with tenants and industry peers recognizing its innovative take on shared living.

Through its commitment to soft femininity, Property Daughters demonstrates that co-living can be both elegant and empowering, offering tenants a truly elevated living experience.

◆ ◆ ◆

Digital Marketing Strategies for Co-Living Spaces

A strong online presence is critical for reaching potential tenants. Digital marketing allows you to connect with your target audience effectively and showcase your properties in the best light.

Search Engine Optimization (SEO)

Optimize your website for search engines to increase visibility. Conduct keyword research to identify terms your audience uses when searching for co-living spaces, such as "affordable co-living near me" or "shared housing for young professionals." Incorporate these keywords naturally into your content, including property descriptions, blog posts, and metadata.

Ensure your website is user-friendly, mobile-optimized, and fast-loading. These factors improve the user experience and contribute to higher search rankings.

Social Media Marketing

Social media is a powerful tool for engaging with potential tenants. Platforms like Instagram, Facebook, and LinkedIn allow you to showcase your properties, share tenant stories, and promote events. Visual content, such as photos and videos, performs particularly well, so focus on creating eye-catching posts that highlight the lifestyle your co-living spaces offer.

Engage with your audience by responding to comments, running polls, and hosting Q&A sessions. Building a strong social media presence fosters a sense of community and keeps your brand top of mind.

Email Campaigns

Email marketing remains one of the most cost-effective ways to communicate with potential tenants. Build a mailing list through your website and offer valuable content, such as tips for co-living success or exclusive promotions. Regular newsletters keep your audience informed about available units, upcoming events, and updates to your properties.

Pay-Per-Click (PPC) Advertising

PPC advertising, such as Google Ads or social media ads, can quickly increase visibility. Target specific demographics, such as young professionals in your city, and drive traffic to your website or property listings. Set a budget and track your ad performance to ensure a strong return on investment.

Networking and Partnerships for Tenant Acquisition

Building partnerships with local businesses and organizations can enhance your marketing efforts and attract tenants. For example, collaborate with universities, coworking spaces, or fitness centers to tap into their networks. Offer exclusive discounts or co-host events to strengthen these partnerships.

Industry networking is also valuable. Attend real estate conferences and property management workshops to connect with other co-living operators and learn from their experiences. These relationships can lead to collaborations, shared best practices, and new opportunities.

Leveraging Tenant Referrals

Your current tenants can be your most effective marketers. Encourage them to refer friends or colleagues by offering referral incentives, such as rent discounts or gift cards. This not only helps fill vacancies but also fosters a sense of community, as tenants are more likely to refer people who align with your property's values.

From Recognition to Retention: The Power of a Strong Brand

Building a recognizable brand and implementing effective marketing strategies are the cornerstones of success in the co-living industry. In a competitive market, it's not enough to simply offer housing; you need to create a living experience that resonates deeply with your target audience. Defining a unique identity for your co-living properties allows you to communicate your values, set expectations, and foster trust.

Leveraging digital tools, from social media to email campaigns, amplifies your reach and ensures your message is seen by the right people. Strong partnerships with local businesses and community organizations further enhance your property's appeal, adding value for tenants and strengthening your presence in the market.

But the true measure of a successful brand goes beyond attracting tenants—it lies in creating a community where people feel genuinely at home. A well-crafted brand transforms your properties into more than just places to live; they become spaces where tenants build relationships, find support, and thrive together. This sense of belonging not only fills vacancies but also encourages long-term residency, turning tenants into loyal advocates for your co-living business.

By focusing on both branding and marketing, you lay the groundwork for a sustainable and impactful co-living enterprise—one that stands out, thrives, and makes a lasting difference in the lives of its residents.

CHAPTER 10

TENANT SATISFACTION AND A THRIVING COMMUNITY CULTURE

"Alone we can do so little; together we can do so much."

— *Helen Keller*

Tenant satisfaction is the cornerstone of a successful co-living business. When tenants feel valued, heard, and part of a thriving community, they're more likely to stay long-term, reducing turnover and fostering a positive environment. This chapter will explore strategies for maintaining tenant satisfaction, addressing conflicts proactively, and building a strong sense of community that enhances the co-living experience.

The Importance of Community in Co-Living

In co-living, the sense of community often defines the tenant experience. Unlike traditional rental setups where neighbors might barely interact, co-living spaces are designed to encourage relationships and shared experiences. This community aspect transforms a property from a mere living space into a home where tenants feel connected and supported.

A strong community provides tenants with a sense of belonging, especially important in urban environments where isolation can be prevalent. When tenants feel part of a supportive network, their overall well-being improves—they're happier, less stressed, and more engaged in their surroundings. This positive atmosphere not only enriches their daily lives but also fosters pride in the living environment, encouraging them to contribute actively to its upkeep and success.

Beyond emotional well-being, a thriving community enhances the overall living experience by creating opportunities for social interaction and shared learning. Imagine tenants hosting events like cooking classes, book clubs, or yoga sessions. These activities not only build friendships but also add value to the co-living environment, making it a vibrant hub of creativity and collaboration.

A strong community also excels in collective problem-solving. When issues arise, tenants can collaborate to address concerns—whether it's organizing a cleanup day, improving communal spaces, or raising maintenance issues collectively. This sense of shared responsibility fosters cooperation and reduces tenant turnover, as tenants feel invested in the community's success.

Reducing Tenant Turnover: Creating a Space Tenants Don't Want to Leave

Tenant retention starts with satisfaction. A satisfied tenant is more likely to renew their lease, reducing the costs and time associated with finding new occupants. To minimize turnover, focus on creating a living experience that tenants can't imagine leaving.

1. **Exceptional Onboarding**: First impressions matter. Ensure new tenants feel welcomed with a seamless onboarding process that includes a comprehensive orientation to the property and community.

2. **Regular Community Engagement**: Keep tenants engaged with regular communication and opportunities to connect. A tenant who feels integrated into the community is less likely to seek housing elsewhere.

3. **Consistent Maintenance and Upgrades**: Stay ahead of maintenance issues and continually improve the property to show tenants that their comfort and satisfaction are priorities.

Proactively Addressing Conflicts

Conflicts are inevitable in shared living environments, but how they're handled makes all the difference. Addressing disputes early and effectively can prevent minor disagreements from escalating and disrupting the community.

Steps for Effective Conflict Resolution:

- **Create Clear House Rules**: Establish guidelines for communal living, such as quiet hours, guest policies, and shared space usage. Ensure all tenants understand and agree to these rules during onboarding.

- **Encourage Open Communication**: Provide tenants with channels to voice concerns or grievances in a safe and respectful manner.

- **Mediate When Necessary**: Step in as a neutral party to help tenants resolve conflicts. Facilitate discussions that allow all parties to express their viewpoints and work toward a mutually acceptable solution.

When tenants see conflicts resolved fairly and efficiently, they're more likely to trust the management and remain committed to the community.

◆◆◆

Ritu's Community-Building Approach

Ritu, a seasoned PadSplit investor, knew from the start that managing shared spaces meant more than just providing a roof over people's heads. His properties were designed to offer not only affordable housing but also a sense of belonging—a community. To achieve this, Ritu implemented a simple yet powerful strategy: weekly house meetings.

Each week, tenants gathered around the dining table to discuss everything from cleaning schedules and maintenance issues to upcoming events and house rules. Ritu believed these meetings were vital to maintaining harmony in the household.

During one such meeting, the group addressed a recurring issue with the kitchen. Some tenants felt others weren't doing their share of the cleaning. Instead of letting frustration simmer, Ritu encouraged open dialogue. "Let's figure out a system that works for everyone," he suggested. Together, they developed a rotating cleaning schedule, ensuring that everyone contributed equally.

Over time, these meetings became more than just logistical check-ins. Tenants began sharing personal updates, celebrating milestones, and even organizing group outings. The weekly gatherings fostered mutual respect and understanding, reducing the potential for conflicts and improving the overall atmosphere in the house.

Ritu noticed that tenants stayed longer, feeling more invested in the property and each other. The shared responsibility created a sense of pride in their living space, transforming the house from a mere rental property into a true home.

Through these meetings, Ritu successfully demonstrated that proactive communication and community-building were key to the success of co-living spaces. His approach not only resolved conflicts before they escalated but also nurtured a vibrant, supportive community where tenants thrived.

◆ ◆ ◆

Building Tenant Relationships: Communication and Feedback

Strong tenant relationships are built on open, transparent communication. Tenants should feel they have direct lines of communication with management and that their voices are heard.

Establishing Communication Channels

Provide multiple ways for tenants to reach you, whether through a messaging platform, email, or regular office hours. Make sure tenants know you're accessible and approachable for any questions, concerns, or feedback.

Regular Updates and Engagement

Keep tenants informed about what's happening within the property. Send out newsletters or updates on maintenance schedules, community events, or policy changes. This keeps tenants in the loop and reinforces their connection to the community.

Encouraging Feedback

Create a culture where feedback is valued. Use surveys, suggestion boxes, or informal chats to gather input from tenants. When tenants see their suggestions lead to tangible improvements, it boosts their satisfaction and trust in the management.

Prompt and Empathetic Responses

When tenants raise concerns, address them promptly and with empathy. A proactive approach to problem-solving reassures tenants that their comfort and satisfaction are top priorities.

Fostering a Sense of Community

Creating a community culture requires more than providing shared spaces. It's about actively fostering interactions and connections among tenants.

Celebrate Milestones

Recognize tenant birthdays, lease anniversaries, or other personal milestones with small gestures like cards or community shout-outs. These touches make tenants feel valued and appreciated.

♦ ♦ ♦

Sweet Gestures

Every few weeks, residents in Macarena's co-living properties look forward to a special surprise. On routine cleaning days, a box of fresh donuts arrives at each house, accompanied by a handwritten thank-you card. The note, signed by Macarena, reads: "Thank you for helping keep our shared home clean and welcoming. Your effort makes our community thrive!"

This small gesture not only brings smiles but also reinforces the sense of appreciation and belonging Macarena strives to cultivate. It's her way of reminding residents that their contributions matter and that they're valued members of a shared community. The donuts quickly disappear, but the positive vibes linger, making cleaning days just a bit sweeter.

♦ ♦ ♦

Highlight Community Contributions

Publicly acknowledge tenants who contribute positively to the community, such as organizing events or maintaining communal areas. This reinforces a culture of cooperation and pride.

Building Long-Term Tenant Relationships

Maintaining tenant satisfaction and fostering a strong community culture are essential for the long-term success of your co-living properties. By proactively addressing conflicts, encouraging open communication, and creating opportunities for tenants to connect, you can reduce turnover and build a thriving, harmonious community. A well-managed co-living space becomes more than just a place to live—it becomes a home where tenants feel valued, supported, and inspired to stay.

CHAPTER 11

NAVIGATING EVICTIONS AND TENANT RIGHTS

"Whenever you are confronted with an opponent, conquer him with love."
— Mahatma Gandhi

Evictions are among the most challenging aspects of property management, particularly in the co-living space, where community dynamics and shared living arrangements add complexity. While no landlord or property manager wants to resort to eviction, being prepared and understanding tenant rights is critical to protecting your investment and maintaining a peaceful community. This chapter explores the eviction process, the importance of tenant rights, and how to navigate this difficult terrain with professionalism and empathy—all while emphasizing that local jurisdiction laws govern the specifics of evictions.

Understanding the Legal Framework of Evictions

Evictions are governed by local laws that dictate the steps landlords must take when removing a tenant. These laws ensure that both landlords and tenants are treated fairly, and following them to the letter is essential. The eviction process typically involves the following steps:

1. **Issuing a Formal Notice**

    The first step is serving a notice to the tenant that they must vacate the property. This notice, often called a "notice to quit" or "notice to vacate," must comply with local laws, including the reasons for eviction and the timeframe for compliance.

    Common reasons for eviction include:

    - Non-payment of rent.
    - Violation of lease terms (e.g., unauthorized occupants or excessive noise).
    - Illegal activities on the property.

2. **Rectifying the Situation**

    Many jurisdictions allow tenants to remedy the situation during the notice period. For example, a tenant facing eviction for non-payment of rent may pay the overdue amount to avoid further action. Open communication can be a powerful tool here. Empathy and understanding often lead to resolutions that benefit both parties.

Tool to Use: Consider providing tenants with written documentation of their options to remedy the situation, such as a payment plan template or a summary of lease terms.

3. **Filing for Eviction in Court**

If the tenant fails to comply with the notice, the next step is filing an eviction lawsuit with the local court. This process involves submitting evidence, such as lease agreements, payment records, and correspondence.

Resource Tip: Work with an attorney specializing in landlord-tenant law. They can ensure all necessary documentation is in order and guide you through the complexities of local procedures.

4. **Court Proceedings**

During the hearing, both the landlord and tenant present their case. The court will issue a ruling based on the evidence. If the court rules in favor of the landlord, an eviction order will be granted.

5. **Enforcing the Eviction**

Local law enforcement typically oversees the enforcement of eviction orders. It's essential to allow authorities to handle this step to ensure the process is carried out legally and safely.

Respecting Tenant Rights During Evictions

Tenants are entitled to specific protections under the law, and landlords must respect these rights at every stage of the eviction process. Key rights often include:

- **Due Process:** Tenants cannot be evicted without proper notice and the opportunity to challenge the eviction in court.
- **Protection Against Retaliation:** Landlords cannot evict tenants as a form of retaliation for complaints or exercising legal rights.
- **Privacy:** Landlords cannot remove tenants' belongings or change locks without a court order.

Violating these rights can lead to legal repercussions and damage to your reputation. Always consult local regulations to ensure compliance.

Handling Evictions with Professionalism and Empathy

Evictions are inherently stressful but approaching them with professionalism and empathy can de-escalate tensions and preserve relationships.

Example: In a co-living property, a tenant fell behind on rent after losing their job. Instead of proceeding immediately with an eviction, the landlord offered a payment plan and connected the tenant with local resources for financial assistance. While the tenant eventually moved out, they appreciated the landlord's understanding and left the property amicably.

Documenting the Eviction Process

Thorough documentation is your best defense against disputes. Keep detailed records of:

- Notices served and delivery methods.
- Communications with the tenant, including emails and text messages.
- Evidence of lease violations or unpaid rent.
- Court filings and rulings.

These records not only protect your interests but also demonstrate professionalism and adherence to legal requirements.

Tools and Resources for Managing Evictions

Several tools and resources can simplify the eviction process and help you navigate it legally:

1. **Legal Counsel:** Partner with a local attorney who specializes in landlord-tenant law.

2. **Tenant Screening Services:** Use services like TransUnion SmartMove or RentPrep to vet tenants thoroughly before leasing.

3. **Eviction Notice Templates:** Ensure your notices meet local legal standards by using templates provided by legal software platforms like Rocket Lawyer or LegalZoom.

4. **Local Housing Authorities:** Stay informed about tenant rights and local eviction procedures through your jurisdiction's housing authority or landlord association.

Post-Eviction Steps: Protecting Your Property and Community

After an eviction, take steps to minimize disruption and restore harmony within your co-living property:

1. **Property Assessment:** Inspect the unit for damages and make necessary repairs.

2. **Tenant Communication:** Address any concerns from remaining tenants about the eviction process.

3. **Re-tenanting:** Use lessons learned from the eviction to refine your tenant screening process and lease agreements.

Community Focus: After an eviction, consider hosting a meeting or event to reassure tenants and foster a sense of stability within the property. Reinforcing the values of respect and responsibility can help maintain a positive atmosphere.

Navigating Evictions with Care and Confidence

While evictions are an unfortunate part of property management, understanding the legal landscape and respecting tenant rights can make the process smoother and less contentious. By staying informed, maintaining professionalism, and using the right tools, you can handle these situations with confidence while upholding the integrity of your co-living community.

Remember, the ultimate goal is to create a living environment that fosters trust, accountability, and mutual respect—ensuring your property remains a thriving and harmonious space for all residents.

CHAPTER 12

THE FUTURE OF CO-LIVING

"The future belongs to those who believe in the beauty of their dreams."
— *Eleanor Roosevelt*

Co-living has evolved from a niche housing model to a transformative force in the real estate market, addressing modern challenges such as affordability, urban density, and the growing demand for community-oriented living. Looking forward, this asset class is poised for substantial growth, offering investors a wealth of opportunities to innovate, diversify, and scale. This chapter explores how investors can leverage the momentum of co-living to maximize returns and contribute meaningfully to the housing landscape of the future.

Recognizing Market Opportunities in Co-Living

The co-living market is rapidly expanding, with increasing demand across various demographics and regions. By identifying untapped markets, investors can position themselves at the forefront of this growth.

Emerging Markets and Underserved Areas

Traditionally, co-living has thrived in major urban hubs where high living costs and limited housing options have driven demand. However, smaller cities and suburban areas are emerging as promising markets for co-living, fueled by population growth, enhanced infrastructure, and the pursuit of affordability.

Population Growth in Smaller Cities

Many smaller cities and suburban areas are experiencing rapid population increases as residents seek alternatives to the high cost of living in urban centers. These areas attract families, young professionals, and retirees looking for lower housing costs without sacrificing quality of life. Despite this growth, many of these regions lack the diverse and flexible housing options that co-living offers.

Infrastructure Improvements and Connectivity

Advances in transportation and technology have made smaller cities and suburban areas more accessible and livable than ever before. Improved public transit, highways, and digital connectivity allow residents to work remotely or commute to urban hubs with ease. For digital nomads and remote workers, co-living spaces in these areas can provide a cost-effective, community-oriented alternative to traditional rentals.

Affordability and Opportunity

Suburban and smaller city markets often have lower property acquisition costs and fewer zoning restrictions, making them ideal for co-living investments. Additionally, tenants in these areas may value co-living for its affordability and community aspects, especially in regions with limited rental housing inventory.

Example: A co-living operator identified a suburban area near a growing university and medical center. The operator converted a large single-family home into a co-living space tailored to healthcare workers and graduate students. The project filled quickly, as tenants appreciated the combination of affordability, proximity to work, and a supportive living environment.

Creating New Co-Living Niches

These emerging markets also present opportunities to tailor co-living spaces to local demographics. For example:

- **Young Professionals:** Smaller cities with burgeoning tech industries or startups are ideal for co-living spaces with shared workspaces and networking events. These spaces provide not only affordable living options but also opportunities for collaboration and career growth, making them attractive hubs for ambitious professionals seeking connection and innovation.

- **Workforce:** In less urban settings, the workforce of blue-collar workers often includes tradespeople, manufacturing employees, healthcare staff, and service industry professionals who are vital to local economies. These individuals typically seek affordable housing options with convenient access to their workplaces, reliable transportation, and community-focused environments that support their practical and lifestyle needs.

- **Retirees:** Suburban areas with a slower pace of life can attract retirees looking for affordable, community-oriented housing. These spaces can also offer tailored amenities such as shared gardens, wellness programs, and opportunities for social engagement, fostering an active and fulfilling lifestyle in their golden years.

Positioning Co-Living for Success in Non-Urban Markets

To succeed in smaller cities and suburbs, co-living operators must adapt to the unique needs of these communities. This might involve:

- Offering longer leases to appeal to tenants seeking stability.
- Including amenities like outdoor spaces, parking, or family-friendly features.
- Collaborating with local businesses or organizations to integrate co-living spaces into the community.

By strategically expanding into these untapped markets, co-living operators can diversify their portfolios, reach new tenant demographics, and capitalize on the growing demand for innovative housing solutions outside traditional urban environments.

Expanding Co-Living to New Horizons

While young professionals remain a core demographic for co-living spaces, the model's flexibility and affordability have begun attracting a much broader audience. By catering to seniors, digital nomads, and families, investors can expand their portfolios and tap into underserved markets, creating differentiated co-living products that stand out in an increasingly competitive field.

Seniors: Aging with Community

As seniors look for alternatives to traditional retirement housing, co-living offers an affordable and socially engaging option. Many older adults seek community-focused environments where they can maintain their independence while enjoying the benefits of shared resources and companionship.

Opportunities:

- Design properties with senior-friendly features like single-level layouts, grab bars, and accessible kitchens.
- Offer amenities such as wellness programs, shared gardens, and spaces for hobbies or group activities.
- Create opportunities for intergenerational interaction, which can enrich the living experience for all residents.

Digital Nomads: Living and Working Anywhere

The rise of remote work has given digital nomads the freedom to live and work wherever they choose, creating a demand for flexible housing options. Co-living spaces tailored to this group can combine affordability with functionality, offering a perfect balance for those on the move.

Opportunities:

- Incorporate co-working spaces with reliable high-speed internet, private meeting rooms, and creative work environments.
- Provide flexible lease options to accommodate short-term stays or periodic relocations.
- Foster a global community by hosting networking events or skill-sharing workshops that attract professionals from various industries.

Multi-Generational Living: The Best of All Worlds

Multi-generational co-living spaces bring together diverse age groups under one roof, fostering unique opportunities for learning and collaboration. These properties can serve a mix of seniors, professionals, and families, creating vibrant communities that thrive on shared experiences.

Opportunities:

- Design properties with flexible layouts that can adapt to diverse needs, such as private suites for seniors and larger units for families.
- Focus on shared amenities that appeal to all generations, like fitness centers, gardens, and multi-purpose rooms for community events.
- Encourage mentorship programs where older residents share skills and experiences with younger ones, enriching the community dynamic.

Forward Thinking: Tailoring to Evolving Needs

The success of demographic diversification lies in anticipating and addressing the unique needs of each group. For example, properties designed for digital nomads should prioritize technology and flexibility, while those for families and seniors might focus on accessibility and community support.

Practical Steps for Investors:

1. Conduct market research to understand the preferences and challenges of your target demographics.

2. Partner with local organizations to create programs or services that enhance the living experience for specific groups.

3. Use data analytics to track the performance of different demographic-focused properties and refine your offerings accordingly.

By embracing demographic diversification, investors can not only fill a wider range of housing needs but also strengthen their position in the co-living market. Tailored spaces that reflect the values and lifestyles of diverse tenants will create communities that are both dynamic and sustainable, ensuring long-term success in this evolving asset class.

Scaling Through Strategic Partnerships

Growth in the co-living sector requires collaboration. Partnerships with developers, technology providers, and local communities can accelerate scaling efforts while mitigating risk.

Joint Ventures with Developers: Scaling Co-Living with Strategic Collaboration

Partnering with developers presents a significant opportunity for co-living investors to scale their portfolios more efficiently and cost-effectively. Joint ventures allow investors to tap into developers' expertise, share resources, and execute projects that align with the unique demands of the co-living model. By working together, both parties can streamline construction timelines, optimize property designs, and reduce operational risks.

Benefits of Partnering with Developers

1. **Custom Design for Co-Living**

   Collaborating on projects designed specifically for co-living eliminates the need for retrofitting traditional properties, which can be costly and time intensive. Developers bring the technical know-how to create layouts that maximize space utilization, incorporate shared amenities, and meet regulatory requirements for co-living spaces.

2. **Shared Resources**

   Joint ventures enable investors to pool resources with developers, sharing costs for land acquisition, permits, and construction materials. This reduces the financial burden on each party and allows for larger-scale projects that might otherwise be unattainable.

3. **Streamlined Construction Timelines**

   Developers often have established networks of contractors and suppliers, allowing projects to progress more efficiently. Modular construction techniques, for instance, can expedite timelines and minimize delays, ensuring properties are ready for occupancy sooner.

4. **Access to Expertise**

Developers bring valuable insights into zoning laws, market trends, and construction best practices. Their expertise ensures that co-living projects are designed to meet both tenant needs and local regulations.

◆◆◆

Case Study: Mid-Rise Modular Co-Living Project

An investor in the Midwest partnered with a regional developer to address the growing demand for co-living spaces among young professionals and remote workers. Together, they planned a mid-rise building specifically tailored for co-living, featuring modular units that included private bedrooms, en-suite bathrooms, and shared common areas such as lounges and co-working spaces.

Key Outcomes:

- **Streamlined Construction:** *The use of modular construction reduced building timelines by 30%, allowing the property to be operational within a year.*

- *Cost Savings:* By leveraging the developer's established supplier network, the project achieved a 15% reduction in material costs compared to traditional construction.
- *Tailored Design:* The building included amenities specifically requested by the target demographic, such as high-speed internet, communal kitchens, and outdoor terraces.

The project's success demonstrated the value of collaboration, resulting in high occupancy rates and a model that could be replicated in other markets.

♦ ♦ ♦

How to Approach Joint Ventures with Developers

1. **Define Roles and Responsibilities:** Clearly outline the responsibilities of each party, including financial contributions, project management, and operational oversight. A well-defined partnership agreement minimizes confusion and ensures alignment throughout the project.

2. **Focus on Mutual Goals:** Ensure both the investor and developer share a vision for the project. For co-living spaces, this includes understanding the target demographic, desired amenities, and long-term operational strategies.

3. **Leverage Developer Expertise:** Work with developers experienced in multi-family housing or modular construction, as their expertise will align closely with the requirements of co-living spaces.

4. **Evaluate the Market Together:** Collaborate on market research to identify locations with high demand for co-living. Developers often have insights into emerging markets and can help pinpoint ideal sites for new projects.

5. **Incorporate Flexibility:** Co-living trends evolve, so design properties with adaptability in mind. Modular units, multi-functional spaces, and scalable layouts ensure the property remains relevant over time.

By forming joint ventures with developers, co-living investors can scale faster, reduce costs, and create properties that stand out in an increasingly competitive market. This strategic collaboration not only enhances profitability but also ensures the long-term viability of co-living as a transformative housing solution.

Local Partnerships: Building Community and Unlocking Growth Opportunities

Engaging with local governments and businesses is a powerful strategy for co-living investors seeking to expand their reach and create sustainable projects. Establishing partnerships at the local level not only fosters community support but also provides access to valuable resources, such as tax incentives and zoning flexibility. These collaborations can be instrumental in ensuring the long-term success of co-living spaces.

Enhancing Community Support

One of the challenges of introducing co-living spaces, particularly in less urban areas, is overcoming community resistance. Concerns about density, noise, and the impact on neighborhood dynamics can arise. By proactively engaging with local stakeholders, co-living operators can address these concerns and demonstrate the value their projects bring to the community.

Strategies for Building Support:

- **Host Community Forums:** Organize meetings where residents and local officials can ask questions and provide input. Transparency about the benefits of co-living, such as addressing housing shortages or revitalizing underutilized properties, helps build trust.
- **Collaborate with Local Organizations:** Partner with nonprofits, workforce development agencies, or community groups to align your co-living space with local needs. For

example, offering priority housing for essential workers can position your project as a community asset.

Leveraging Public-Private Partnerships (PPPs)

Public-private partnerships offer co-living investors unique opportunities to collaborate with local governments on projects that align with community development goals. These partnerships can unlock resources and incentives that significantly reduce costs and streamline the approval process.

Key Benefits of PPPs:

1. **Tax Incentives:** Governments often provide tax abatements or credits for projects that contribute to affordable housing or community improvement.

2. **Zoning Flexibility:** Collaborating with local authorities can lead to zoning adjustments that make co-living developments feasible in areas where they might not typically be allowed.

3. **Access to Public Resources:** Partnerships may grant access to publicly owned land or funding for infrastructure improvements.

Example: A co-living investor partnered with a local government to repurpose a vacant school building into a co-living space. The city provided zoning changes and tax incentives, while the investor transformed the property into a vibrant community hub with shared amenities and affordable housing options.

Partnering with Local Businesses

Engaging with local businesses can enhance the tenant experience while integrating your co-living property into the broader community. Partnerships with nearby companies can create mutually beneficial opportunities that support both tenants and the local economy.

Ideas for Business Partnerships:

- **Workforce Housing Solutions:** Collaborate with local employers to provide housing for their employees. This is especially beneficial in areas with workforce shortages, such as healthcare or manufacturing hubs.
- **Exclusive Tenant Discounts:** Partner with nearby cafes, gyms, or coworking spaces to offer residents exclusive discounts, enhancing the value of your co-living space.
- **Local Service Providers:** Work with local businesses to offer services like housekeeping, catering, or fitness classes directly to tenants, creating convenience and fostering economic ties.

Navigating Regulatory Incentives

Many local governments are keen to address housing shortages and may offer regulatory incentives for co-living developments. These incentives not only reduce operational hurdles but also improve project feasibility.

Steps to Access Incentives:

1. **Engage Early:** Meet with local planning and zoning officials early in the development process to understand potential incentives and ensure your project aligns with community goals.

2. **Demonstrate Impact:** Highlight how your co-living project addresses local housing challenges, such as affordability or workforce accommodation.

3. **Stay Involved:** Participate in local housing initiatives or economic development programs to maintain strong relationships with decision-makers.

Example: In a fast-growing suburban area, an investor received expedited permitting and reduced impact fees by committing to include affordable co-living units in their development.

The Long-Term Value of Local Partnerships

Fostering strong relationships with local governments and businesses creates a foundation for sustainable growth. Beyond immediate benefits like incentives or zoning flexibility, these partnerships position co-living investors as valued contributors to the community.

By engaging with local stakeholders, co-living operators can ensure their projects meet the needs of residents, gain community buy-in, and establish themselves as trusted partners in solving housing challenges. This collaborative approach not only enhances the success of individual properties but also strengthens the reputation of co-living as a vital housing solution.

Innovating Business Models: Redefining the Future of Co-Living

The evolution of co-living is driven by the need for adaptability and creativity in business models. As the housing landscape changes, operators who embrace innovation can differentiate themselves and capture untapped market segments. Experimenting with varied approaches—such as offering flexible lease terms, multi-generational living arrangements, or niche-targeted communities—can attract a broader range of tenants while addressing emerging lifestyle trends. For example, implementing subscription-based models, where residents pay an all-inclusive fee for rent, utilities, and amenities, simplifies the tenant experience and provides a predictable revenue stream for operators. This innovative model also aligns with tenants' desire for convenience and transparency, enhancing satisfaction and retention.

Expanding revenue streams is equally critical in a competitive market. Co-living operators can diversify income by incorporating value-added services such as high-speed internet packages, or premium amenities like lounges and co-working spaces. Partnerships with local businesses, such as cafes or wellness providers, can create additional offerings for residents while fostering community ties. Furthermore, operators can explore integrating technology-driven solutions, such as app-based maintenance requests or virtual tours, to streamline operations and reduce costs. By continually testing and refining these innovations, co-living operators can position their properties as dynamic, future-ready spaces that appeal to the evolving needs of tenants and maximize long-term profitability.

Subscription-Based Living

Using platforms like PadSplit can significantly streamline operations and accelerate growth in the co-living space. PadSplit's comprehensive tools handle much of the administrative burden, including tenant screening, payment collection, and maintenance coordination, allowing investors to focus on scaling their portfolio.

With its proven membership model, PadSplit attracts tenants seeking flexibility while providing operators with predictable revenue streams and a supportive community network. By utilizing a platform like PadSplit, you can reduce operational complexities and position your co-living properties for sustainable, scalable success.

Elevating the Co-Living Experience with Premium Amenities

Incorporating high-quality amenities can set your co-living properties apart from the competition and attract tenants willing to pay a premium for an elevated living experience. Properties located in nice neighborhoods with access to walkable spaces, parks and recreation centers, transit options, and entertainment hubs are particularly appealing.

Inside the property, high-end finishes such as granite countertops, stainless steel appliances, and premium flooring create a sense of luxury and comfort. Fully furnished spaces with stylish and durable furniture add to the appeal, allowing tenants to move in seamlessly.

Shared spaces are equally critical for enhancing tenant satisfaction. Cozy lounges, shared workspaces equipped with fast Wi-Fi, and outdoor porches or decks offer both functionality and relaxation.

These amenities foster a sense of community while providing spaces for tenants to work, socialize, or unwind.

By focusing on these premium features, you can attract a broader demographic, including professionals and digital nomads, while boosting tenant retention and overall revenue.

Impact Investing

As the co-living model evolves, its ability to address critical social challenges—such as housing affordability, urban density, and community-building—makes it an attractive investment for socially conscious stakeholders. Investors focused on ESG (Environmental, Social, Governance) criteria are particularly drawn to opportunities that align profitability with purpose, and co-living offers a compelling case for both.

Co-living is uniquely positioned to tackle the affordability crisis, providing flexible, cost-effective housing options for individuals who might otherwise struggle in traditional rental markets. By optimizing shared spaces and leveraging economies of scale, co-living reduces per-tenant costs while maintaining quality and convenience. Highlighting your property's role in making housing accessible—especially in high-cost urban areas—can resonate deeply with impact-focused investors.

Example: A co-living property in a rapidly gentrifying neighborhood could partner with local organizations to prioritize affordable options for essential workers, such as teachers and healthcare professionals. Such initiatives demonstrate a commitment to social equity, making the property attractive to ESG investors.

Preparing for Regulatory Evolution: Navigating the Future of Co-Living

As the co-living model gains momentum, it is drawing increasing attention from regulators who aim to balance innovation with community standards. This evolving oversight presents both challenges and opportunities for investors. Proactively addressing regulatory hurdles and building adaptable strategies will help co-living operators not only comply with changing rules but also thrive in a dynamic environment.

Engaging with Policymakers

Advocacy is crucial in shaping favorable co-living regulations. By participating in industry organizations, housing forums, and local discussions, investors can influence policies that align with the unique needs of co-living communities. Establishing relationships with policymakers and city planners allows operators to provide insights into the benefits of co-living, such as affordability, efficient use of space, and community building.

Actionable Steps:

- Attend city council meetings or housing summits to remain informed about regulatory discussions.
- Join industry groups like real estate investor associations or co-living networks to strengthen your voice in policy advocacy.
- Partner with other stakeholders to present data-driven arguments showcasing how co-living addresses housing challenges.

By fostering these connections, investors can advocate for clear, supportive regulations and preemptively address concerns from local authorities or neighbors.

Adapting to Zoning Changes

Zoning laws remain one of the most significant barriers to co-living expansion. Many municipalities have yet to update their zoning codes to accommodate the shared housing model, often categorizing co-living properties as multi-family or boarding houses. Staying informed about zoning trends and preparing to adapt properties accordingly can prevent costly delays or operational roadblocks.

Strategies for Adapting:

- **Seeking Variances:** In areas where zoning laws restrict co-living, applying for variances or special-use permits can help secure approvals. This process often involves demonstrating community benefits and addressing potential concerns, such as traffic or density.
- **Repositioning Assets:** If zoning changes make certain properties untenable for co-living, consider alternative uses such as short-term rentals, workforce housing, or boutique accommodations to maintain profitability.

Engaging early with zoning boards and legal experts ensures compliance while preserving flexibility for future projects.

Building a Resilient Co-Living Portfolio

The key to thriving amid regulatory evolution is diversification. Spreading investments across different regions, demographics, and business models mitigates risks associated with localized regulatory changes or economic fluctuations. For example, an investor with properties in both urban and suburban markets can better withstand market shifts than one concentrated in a single area.

Financial Sustainability

Regulatory changes can impact costs, rental pricing, and operational efficiency. Conducting regular financial reviews ensures that your portfolio remains profitable despite evolving legal landscapes.

Best Practices:

- Monitor key financial metrics, such as cash flow, ROI, and occupancy rates.
- Develop contingency budgets for potential compliance upgrades, such as retrofitting properties to meet new safety standards.
- Seek guidance from financial advisors or accountants familiar with real estate to optimize tax strategies and long-term planning.

By aligning financial sustainability with compliance efforts, you create a foundation for steady growth.

Future-Proofing Properties

Preparing for regulatory evolution also involves designing properties that remain relevant and compliant as housing trends and laws change. Investing in features like modular construction, energy efficiency, and flexible layouts ensures that your properties can adapt to a variety of scenarios.

Examples of Future-Proofing:

- **Modular Construction:** Easily reconfigure layouts to meet changing occupancy rules or tenant preferences.
- **Sustainability Initiatives:** Incorporate solar panels, energy-efficient appliances, and water-saving fixtures to align with environmental regulations and appeal to eco-conscious tenants.
- **Flexible Use:** Create multi-functional spaces that can serve as private units, shared amenities, or co-working areas, depending on tenant demand or legal requirements.

Future-proofing not only ensures compliance but also enhances tenant satisfaction and operational efficiency.

Proactive Strategies for a Changing Landscape

Navigating the regulatory evolution of co-living requires a proactive and adaptable mindset. By engaging with policymakers, staying informed about zoning trends, and building a diversified and financially sound portfolio, investors can position themselves for success. Future-proofing properties with sustainable, flexible designs ensures long-term relevance, even as laws and tenant needs evolve.

Rather than viewing regulations as obstacles, treat them as opportunities to refine your operations and demonstrate the value of co-living to communities and governments alike. With foresight and preparation, your co-living investments can thrive in a rapidly changing housing landscape.

The Thriving Future of Co-Living

The co-living industry is poised for explosive growth, driven by demographic shifts, technological advancements, and evolving lifestyle preferences. By staying ahead of trends, embracing innovation, and building strategic partnerships, investors can capitalize on this dynamic asset class and create lasting value.

Co-living is more than a housing model—it's a solution to some of the most pressing challenges of modern life. By leveraging its potential, you're not only positioning yourself for financial success but also contributing to a brighter, more connected future in housing. Embrace the possibilities and take the next step toward scaling your co-living portfolio into a thriving, future-ready enterprise.

CONCLUSION

YOUR JOURNEY AS A CO-LIVING INVESTOR BEGINS

"Do what you can, with what you have, where you are."
— Theodore Roosevelt

First, let me say congratulations! Reaching the end of this book is a significant achievement, and it shows your commitment to learning and growing. By choosing to explore the co-living model, you're not just setting yourself apart as an investor—you're stepping into a movement that blends innovation, purpose, and profitability. You've taken a vital first step toward addressing the affordable housing crisis while building a thriving investment portfolio.

Co-living is more than a business model; it's about creating spaces where people feel a sense of community and belonging. As someone who's seen how co-living transforms lives and builds connections, I'm thrilled to know you're ready to embrace this opportunity. The strategies and insights in this book are meant to guide you, but ultimately, it's your vision and action that will bring these ideas to life.

This journey is about more than real estate—it's about creating meaningful change. Co-living offers you the chance to provide affordable, dignified housing while creating spaces where people can connect, grow, and thrive. For women investors especially, this is a moment to step into a traditionally male-dominated industry and lead with your unique perspective and capabilities. The co-living space is ripe for innovation, and your voice is needed now more than ever.

Feeling uncertain as you begin is natural. Every worthwhile journey comes with its challenges, but you're equipped with the knowledge to take the first step. Remember, action is what sets successful investors apart—start small if you need to, but start. Progress, no matter how incremental, adds up, and the confidence you build will carry you forward.

I can't stress enough the importance of staying curious and committed to learning. The co-living landscape, like all real estate markets, is ever-changing. Trends shift, technologies emerge, and new challenges arise. By staying informed, connecting with other investors, and seeking out resources, you'll keep yourself ahead of the curve. Real estate investment groups, online forums, and conferences can provide valuable insights and connections as you continue to grow.

Above all, let your purpose guide you. Co-living isn't just a financial opportunity; it's a chance to create positive change in the world. When you prioritize the well-being of your residents, your investments will thrive, and you'll experience a deeper sense of fulfillment. Building homes—not just housing—means fostering environments where people feel safe, valued, and supported.

To the women investors reading this: I hope this book has ignited your belief in your ability to drive change. This is your time to make your mark in real estate and to inspire others to follow your lead. Your success will ripple outward, empowering more women to see themselves as leaders and innovators in this space.

As you move forward, remember that every investment is a learning opportunity. There will be highs and lows, but each experience will strengthen your knowledge and resolve. Don't be afraid to take risks, trust your instincts, and lean on mentors and peers who can support and guide you. Finding a mentor who understands the unique challenges and rewards of co-living can make all the difference, so don't hesitate to reach out to those you admire.

You now have the tools, strategies, and insights to embark on your co-living journey. You have the power to create homes that transform lives, including your own. Thank you for trusting me to guide you through this exploration of co-living investments. I hope this book has inspired you to think differently about what's possible in real estate and encouraged you to step into your full potential.

Your journey doesn't end here—it's just beginning. Stay curious, stay committed, and above all, stay courageous. The future of co-living is bright, and I can't wait to see the incredible impact you'll make. Congratulations again, and I'll be cheering you on every step of the way.

REFERENCES

Gollom, D. J. (2019). The Co-Living Code: How to Build a Successful Co-Living Space. New York, NY: Real Estate Press.

Shaffer, K. (2021). Creating Communities: How Shared Spaces are Changing the Way We Live and Work. London, UK: Urban Life Publishers.

Davis, L. & Peterson, M. (2020). Sustainable Living in Urban Spaces: Innovations and Strategies for Co-Living and Co-Working Environments. Boston, MA: Green Future Publishing.

Larson, E. (2018). Real Estate Investing for Women: Strategies to Build Wealth through Co-Living and Shared Spaces. San Francisco, CA: Women in Business Press.

Richards, J. (2022). The Future of Housing: Co-Living and the Shift to Shared Spaces. Cambridge, UK: Global Urban Studies.

Zhang, T. (2020). Affordable Housing Strategies: Bridging the Gap through Innovative Solutions. New York, NY: Housing Innovation Press.

Green, P. (2017). Co-Living: The New Urban Living Revolution. Los Angeles, CA: Urban Development Publishing.

Turner, W. (2019). Building Wealth through Real Estate Investment: A Guide for Women. Chicago, IL: Empowered Investing Press.

Nelson, A. (2021). Shared Spaces and Sustainable Communities: The Rise of Co-Living. Washington, DC: Urban Sustainability Publications.

Ford, M. (2018). From Concept to Reality: Developing Successful Co-Living Spaces. Houston, TX: Real Estate Visionaries.

Wilson, J. (2022). Creating Affordable Housing Solutions: Strategies for a Better Future. London, UK: Global Housing Press.

International Co-Living Association. (2022, December 10). Building a Successful Co-Living Space: Tips and Best Practices. https://www.colivingassociation.org/building-successful-coliving

Urban Land Institute. (2021, October 15). Trends in Co-Living Spaces and Their Impact on Real Estate. https://www.uli.org/trends-in-coliving-spaces

Sustainable Living Guide. (2022, August 22). Eco-Friendly Practices in Co-Living Communities. SustainableLivingGuide.com. https://www.sustainablelivingguide.com/eco-friendly-practices-coliving

National Housing Institute. (2023, January 19). Affordable Housing Solutions: The Rise of Co-Living. NationalHousingInstitute.org. https://www.nhi.org/affordable-housing-coliving

Co-Living Network. (2023, February 10). How to Maximize Rental Income from Co-Living Spaces. CoLivingNetwork.org. https://www.colivingnetwork.org/maximize-rental-income

Green Housing Initiative. (2021, November 30). Sustainable Co-Living: Reducing Environmental Impact. GreenHousingInitiative.com. https://www.greenhousinginitiative.com/sustainable-coliving

Affordable Housing Online. (2022, July 5). The Role of Co-Living in Tackling the Housing Crisis. AffordableHousingOnline.org. https://www.affordablehousingonline.org/coliving-role

Women in Real Estate Foundation. (2023, April 9). Empowering Women Investors in Co-Living Ventures. WomenInRealEstate.org. https://www.womeninrealestate.org/coliving-investors

Real Estate Innovations. (2022, May 14). Future Trends in Co-Living Spaces. RealEstateInnovations.com. https://www.realestateinnovations.com/future-coliving-trends

Housing Policy Watch. (2022, September 25). Navigating Legal Challenges in Co-Living Arrangements. HousingPolicyWatch.org. https://www.housingpolicywatch.org/legal-challenges

Tenant Resource Center. (2023, June 17). Understanding Tenant Rights in Co-Living Spaces. TenantResourceCenter.com. https://www.tenantresourcecenter.com/rights-coliving

Co-Living Innovators. (2022, December 8). Digital Marketing Strategies for Co-Living Properties. CoLivingInnovators.com. https://www.colivinginnovators.com/digital-marketing

The Urbanist. (2021, October 12). How Technology is Shaping the Future of Co-Living. TheUrbanist.com. https://www.theurbanist.com/technology-coliving

Investment in Green Spaces. (2023, January 7). Eco-Friendly Real Estate Investments. InvestmentInGreenSpaces.com. https://www.investmentingreenspaces.com/eco-friendly-investments

ABOUT THE AUTHOR

Macarena García is a seasoned real estate investor, educator, and advocate for innovative housing solutions. Based in the metro Atlanta area, she has been investing in and managing rental properties since 2009, beginning her journey in Anaheim, California. With a portfolio of over a dozen mid-term rental and co-living properties, Macarena is dedicated to addressing the affordable housing crisis while creating thriving, community-focused living spaces.

As a mentor and coach, Macarena empowers women to break into the real estate industry and succeed in co-living investments. She is passionate about combining profitability with purpose, inspiring others to create homes that foster belonging and connection. Through her work, she continues to drive positive change in the housing market, one community at a time.

PadSplit Masterclass
Macarena Garcia

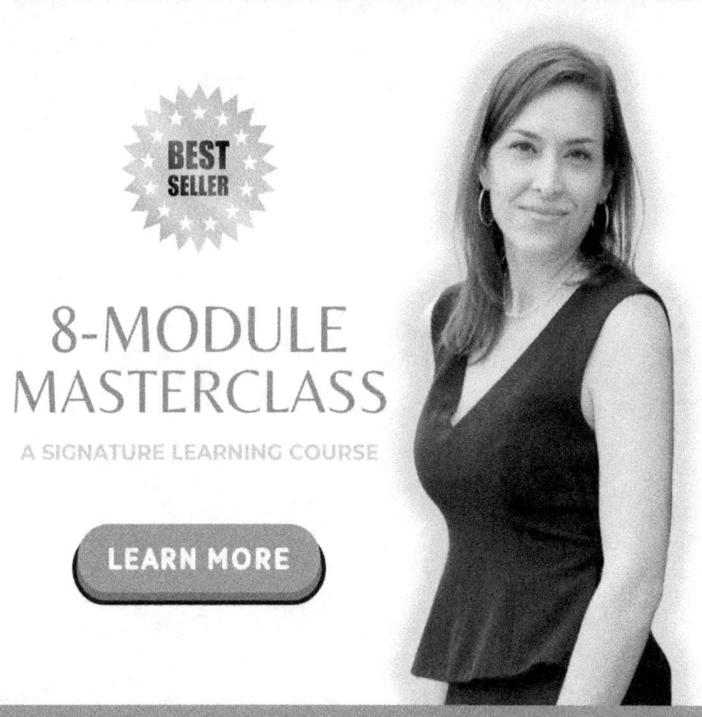

BEST SELLER
8-MODULE MASTERCLASS
A SIGNATURE LEARNING COURSE
LEARN MORE
WomenWiseAcademy.com